THRIVE

30 Inspirational Rags-to-Riches Stories

JASON NAVALLO

TABLE OF CONTENTS

INTRODUCTION

S uccess is a lifelong pursuit. It is a journey that will take you through many ups and downs, twists and turns. If you are ambitious and want to achieve greatness, then this book is for you. Whether you're an entrepreneur promoting a product or service, an employee climbing the corporate ladder, or someone seeking motivation to reach new heights in your career and life, you are in the right place.

In this book, you will uncover the rags-to-riches stories of thirty wealthy entrepreneurs, innovative businessmen, and famous artists. Although society admires their successes, their struggles to initially establish and build their careers are often overlooked. The truth is that through sheer will and determination, these people transformed their visions into realities. Nothing was handed to them, and, more importantly, they never gave up.

This book will inspire you to achieve what you want in life, regardless of your age, occupation, or environment. It will inspire you to believe anything is possible and to believe there are always opportunities for you to succeed. It will give you hope when times are bleak and when you feel like giving up. Everything we desire is within reach, and these thirty people and their inspiring rags-to-riches stories serve as proof. So, read. Learn. Thrive.

JIM CARREY

James "Jim" Carrey was born in Newmarket, Ontario, Canada. The youngest of four children, Jim's father was an accountant and his mother was a homemaker. From an early age, Jim expressed an interest in comedy. By junior high school, he was labeled a class clown and arranged time at the end of each school day to perform in front of his classmates. At age fourteen, Jim attempted stand-up at a local comedy club called Yuk Yuk's in Toronto, Canada, but was booed offstage.

Things took a turn for the worse when his father lost his accounting job, and his family was forced out of their home and moved into a farmhouse on factory grounds. His father found work as a security guard, and Jim and his siblings cleaned the plant at night. When his mother became ill and bedridden, Jim stayed home from school to care for her. His comedy grew tremendously, as Jim often performed to make his mother laugh. His family eventually abandoned the plant and was forced to live in a Volkswagen bus.

At age seventeen, Jim bravely returned to stand-up comedy at Yuk Yuk's. This time, he was determined to overcome the hecklers, and he did. He quickly made a name for himself in the local Toronto comedy circuit, and in a giant leap of faith, Jim moved to Los Angeles, California to pursue his dream of becoming a successful comedian. Shortly after arriving, he wrote himself a check for ten million dollars, for "Acting Services Rendered," later dating it Thanksgiving 1995, giving himself ten years to make it happen. He kept it in his wallet, determined he would be able to cash it one day.

For many months, Jim performed for no pay and no preparation at The Comedy Store on Sunset Boulevard. He worked tirelessly on improving his impersonations routine. The hard work paid off when Rodney Dangerfield caught his show one night and signed him as an opener for an entire season of tour performances. Hollywood began to take notice of him, as Jim appeared on *An Evening at the Improv* and *The Tonight Show.* However, Jim grew wary of being boxed into a lounge act lifestyle, so he shifted his focus on achieving a successful career in television and movies. He auditioned to become a cast member on the American live television comedy show *Saturday Night Live,* but didn't make the cut.

Every night, Jim drove up a hill overlooking Los Angeles and visualized himself as a successful comedian. He visualized himself landing big acting roles and receiving compliments on his work from actors and comedians he respected. Not only did this practice make him feel better, but it also assured him that everything he wanted was going to be in his life. After landing several minor acting roles in movies, and after a brief return to stand-up comedy, where he retired his impersonations routine, Jim landed a role playing the alien Wiploc in *Earth Girls Are Easy* (1988). On set, he worked alongside fellow comedian and actor Damon Wayans, who was impressed with Jim's work. Wayans called his brothers to insist that Jim audition for their sketch comedy show, *In Living Color* (1990-1994). After a successful audition, Jim became a hit on the show, performing as a regular for four seasons, and successfully transformed his image from stand-up comedian to television genius.

Following his success on television, Jim started to receive leading roles in movie projects. He participated in rewriting the screenplay for *Ace Ventura: Pet Detective* (1994), which he also starred in and which became a smash hit at the box office, grossing $107 million worldwide. He followed with starring roles in *The Mask* (1994) and *Dumb & Dumber* (1995), earning enough money to be able to cash that $10 million check in time for Thanksgiving 1995. At his father's funeral in 1994, Jim placed the check into his father's casket, signifying the fulfillment of both of their dreams. He became one of Hollywood's biggest stars, as well as the first actor in the history of cinema to receive $20 million for a movie, which Jim was paid for his role in *The Cable Guy* (1996).

EMINEM

Marshall Bruce "Eminem" Mathers III was born in St. Louis, Missouri. His father abandoned the family when Marshall was an infant, and his mother never held down a job for more than several months at a time. Growing up, Marshall and his mother frequently moved between Missouri and Detroit, Michigan, before settling in Detroit during Marshall's early teenage years. In school, Marshall was often bullied. One bully beat him so hard that he suffered a severe head injury. Even after he recovered, the bullying continued.

Marshall was introduced to hip-hop at the age of nine by his Uncle Ronnie, who was not much older than Marshall. Later, Ronnie committed suicide after a devastating relationship breakup. Marshall started rapping at age fourteen under the pseudonym "M&M," which he later changed to "Eminem." After spending three years in the ninth grade due to truancy and poor grades, Marshall dropped out. He then held a variety of jobs to support his mother with paying the bills, while honing his rapping skills. One of his regular jobs was working as a cook for minimum wage at a local restaurant. Because he was a Caucasian rapper in a predominantly African-American industry and neighborhood, Marshall was, at first, not taken seriously. However, his strong rapping skills eventually won him the respect of the local underground hip-hop community.

As Marshall struggled to establish his rap career, his girlfriend, Kim Scott, gave birth to their daughter, Hailie. The birth forced Marshall to spend less time rapping and more time providing for his family. During this time, the couple and their newborn daughter lived in crack-infested neighborhoods and were often robbed. Under these poor conditions, Marshall began to assemble together his debut album, *Infinite* (1996). Topics on the album include his struggles raising his newborn daughter on limited funds and his strong desire to be wealthy. Unfortunately, the record failed to take off, and Marshall was fired from his cooking job five days before Christmas (which is also Hailie's birthday). His personal struggles with alcohol and drug abuse led to an unsuccessful suicide attempt.

Marshall and his new family then moved into a mobile

home with his mother. Realizing he had to change his approach in order to become a successful rapper, he developed a dark alter ego named "Slim Shady" to voice all of his anger and frustrations in his music. He began work on his next album, *The Slim Shady EP* (1997), which features strong references to drug use, sexual acts, mental instability, and over-the-top violence. The album even makes personal attacks toward Kim and his own mother. It became a hit in the underground community, and Marshall was featured in hip-hop magazine *The Source*'s "Unsigned Hype" column a few months after its release.

As his rap career gained traction, Marshall's personal life deteriorated. After a bitter breakup, Kim took Hailie and moved in with her mother, while Marshall moved in with some friends. The night before he was scheduled to compete in the 1997 Rap Olympics in Los Angeles, California, Marshall came home to a locked door and an eviction notice. With nowhere else to go, Marshall broke into the unheated apartment and slept on the floor. The following morning, he travelled to Los Angeles to compete.

At the freestyling competition, Marshall had his eyes on the grand prize of $500 and a Rolex watch, knowing how much his family needed the money. He gave it his all, and after an intense series of rap battles, he placed second to a local rapper. Afterward, Marshall was approached by an audience member who requested a copy of his demo tape. Marshall gave it to him and thought nothing of it, not knowing that the man worked for Interscope Records, a leading hip-hop record label.

Marshall's demo tape landed in the hands of Interscope Record's CEO, Jimmy Levine, who played it for legendary hip-hop record producer Dr. Dre, who immediately responded, "Find him. Now." A speechless Marshall was flown back to California to meet with Dr. Dre, who he had idolized for many years. After a series of highly-productive recording sessions, Marshall signed to Dr. Dre's record label, Aftermath Entertainment. He introduced himself to the world with his debut, attention-grabbing single "My Name Is" on January 25, 1999, which he recorded in an hour's time with Dr. Dre on their first day in the studio together. The response was overwhelming. He followed with his second studio album and first major release, *The Slim Shady LP* (1999), which has sold over 18 million copies worldwide. His third studio album, *The Marshall Mathers LP* (2000), sold over 1.76 million copies in its first week and over 32 million copies worldwide.

Eminem is widely considered to be one of the greatest artists of all time, as well as the best-selling solo artist of the 2000s in the United States.

SAM WALTON

Samuel "Sam" Walton was born in Kingfisher, Oklahoma. His father held a variety of jobs, including banker, farmer, farm-loan appraiser, and insurance and real estate agent, while his mother was a homemaker. Growing up during the Great Depression, Sam performed many chores to help his family make ends meet, including milking the family cow and delivering milk bottles to customers after school.

After high school, Sam attended the University of Missouri, where he also played on the football team. As his parents could not afford to pay for his tuition, Sam paid his way through college on his own. He held various jobs, including waiting tables (in exchange for meals), working as a lifeguard, delivering newspapers, and selling magazine subscriptions. By the end of college, Sam had employees and was earning $4,000 to $5,000 per year, a respectable amount at the time. When Sam ran for student body president, he learned the secret to winning votes that would later serve him well working in retail: speak to people coming down the sidewalk before they speak to you. He went out of his way to get to know everyone on campus, and everyone thought of Sam as their friend. As a result, he was successful in being elected to every office he ran for.

When he graduated with a business degree, Sam planned on becoming an insurance salesman. However, after speaking with a couple of college recruiters from J.C. Penney and Sears Roebuck, Sam decided to pursue a career in retail. He accepted a job as a management trainee with J.C. Penney in Des Moine, Iowa for a starting salary of $75 per month. He proved to be a good salesman, with one problem: his handwriting was terrible. Sam also couldn't stand making a customer wait while he was going through paperwork, which caused great confusion for the store's back office. "Walton, I'd fire you if you weren't such a good salesman. Maybe you're just not cut out for retail," said his J.C. Penney regional manager, Phil Blake.

Sam quit his job at J.C. Penney after eighteen months to join the United States Armed Forces during World War II. However, he was turned down for combat due to a minor heart irregularity. Since he already quit his job, Sam headed south to Tulsa, Oklahoma to find a job in the booming oil business. There, he met his wife, Helen Robson. Before the two could marry, Sam was called by the U.S. Army Intelligence Corps to serve, supervising security at aircraft plants and POW camps across the United States. He married Helen on Valentine's Day the following year.

While serving, Sam kept his passion for the retail business, reading books to educate himself and studying retail businesses across the country. Sam's father-in-law was a prominent lawyer, banker, and rancher who recognized Sam's potential. After the war, Sam approached the Butler Brothers Company, which operated two chains of franchise retail stores: Federated Stores and Ben Franklin. The company offered twenty-seven-year-old Sam a Ben Franklin store of his own in Newport, Arkansas. Borrowing $20,000 from his father-in-law and investing $5,000 of his own money, Sam agreed to pay 5 percent of gross sales as rent and bought the store, which at the time grossed around $72,000 in sales per year. As Sam believed in setting goals, he set a goal for this store: he wanted it to be the best, most profitable variety store in Arkansas within five years.

Sam succeeded in growing the store's sales figures. He tried a lot of promotional tactics to do so, even taking a $1,800 loan from the bank to buy a soft ice cream machine for the front of the store, which ultimately became very profitable. Within three years, Sam grew sales from $72,000 to $175,000, and he was able to pay back his father-in-law. Sam also managed to take over the lease for the store adjacent to his competitor across the street, which prevented his competitor from expanding his store. After five years, Sam's store was turning over $250,000 in gross sales per year, with $40,000 in profits. Phil Blake, Sam's former manager at J.C. Penney, almost fell over when he heard of Sam's success. "It can't be the same one I knew in Des Moines," he said. "That fellow couldn't have amounted to anything."

Sam's eagerness to get started in business was so strong that he failed to negotiate a right-of-renewal clause in his lease. As a result, his landlord refused to renew the lease because he wanted to buy Sam's store for his own son. Sam had no other option but to sell his store and start somewhere else, taking everything he learned over the past five years. It was the lowest point of his business career. He became sick to his stomach, as he had to move his devastated family out of town. On the way out, however, Sam sold the lease to his competitor, which allowed him to finally expand.

At thirty-two years old, Sam found a small store to take over in Bentonville, Arkansas that was grossing roughly $32,000 per year. He negotiated a ninety-nine-year lease on the store and the barber shop next to it. After reading a newspaper article about two Ben Franklin franchises in Minnesota who switched to "self-service," a new retail concept at the time, Sam rode the bus all night long to check out the two stores. He liked what he saw and decided to create a large store around the "self-service" concept, calling it Walton's Five and Dime, although it operated as a Ben Franklin franchise. He "just had a personality that drew people in. He would yell at you from a block away, you know. He would just yell at everyone he saw, and that's the reason so many liked him and did business in the store. It was like he brought in business by his being so friendly," said Inex Threet, a clerk who once worked at Walton's Five and Dime.

Learning from the past, Sam knew not to put all of his eggs in one basket. He, along with his brother, reinvested their profits to open more Ben Franklin franchises in various locations. Sam had driven so much (between stores) that he bought a small used airplane in order to save time. Within fifteen years, Sam had become the largest independent variety store owner in the United States, with fifteen stores and a turnover of $1.4 million per year. However, Sam felt the business was limited and the "volume was so little for each store that it really didn't amount to that much."

Sam noticed that "discounting" would become the new wave in the retail industry. He knew that large discount centers would devastate the variety store business. After travelling across the country studying the discounting concept, Sam knew he had to act. He approached the

Butler Brothers and requested they back him on his new discounting venture. However, the brothers weren't interested. Nobody wanted to gamble on the first Wal-Mart store in Rogers, Arkansas. Sam's brother Bud contributed 3 percent of the costs and the new store manager, Don Whitaker, contributed 2 percent, while Sam and his wife, Helen, contributed 95 percent.

The first Wal-Mart opened its doors to a crowd of shoppers on July 2, 1962. However, not everyone was happy about the grand opening. A group of "officials" from Ben Franklin in Chicago paid Sam a visit and gave him an ultimatum to not open any more stores. The first Wal-Mart turned out to be moderately successful, eventually grossing over $1 million per year, in a town with a population of less than 6,000 people. Here's what Sam had to say about the opening:

"Once we opened that Wal-Mart in Springdale, I knew we were on to something. I knew in my bones it was going to work. But at the time, most folks—including my brother Bud—were pretty skeptical of the whole concept. They thought Wal-Mart was just another one of my crazy ideas. It was totally unproven at the time, but it was really just what we'd been doing all along: experimenting, trying to do something different, educating ourselves as to what was going on in the retail industry, and trying to stay ahead of those trends. This is a big contradiction in my makeup that I don't completely understand to this day. In many of my core values I'm very conservative. But for some reason, in business I have always been driven to buck the system, to innovate, to take things beyond where they've been."

The discounting concept took off quickly, and Wal-Mart competed with other discount retailers, including Kmart, which established 250 stores with $800 million in sales within five years. Wal-Mart, at the time, had just 19 stores with $9 million in sales. Sam continued to be laser-focused on growth. He was committed to passing down savings to his customers and refused to markup products more than 30 percent. At the time, Sam knew the key to expanding his empire was to build a solid support structure with a close-knit management team and efficient distribution channels. At first, each manager ordered merchandise separately, which was delivered directly to the store from the manufacturer. However, Sam realized it was more efficient to have a centralized warehouse, which would allow him to secure a better price by buying in bulk.

To fund growth so far, Sam and his wife had borrowed money from almost every bank in Arkansas and Missouri. They were millions of dollars in debt, and Sam always worried that if all of their loans were called in at the same time, Wal-Mart would be forced out of business. The best thing to do, Sam realized, was to take his company public by having his company's shares listed on a stock exchange. Wal-Mart Stores, Inc. went public on October 1, 1970, offering 300,000 shares at $16.50, and freed Sam of his worries about debt. He focused on putting large discount stores into small towns. Within ten years, Wal-Mart's sales jumped from $31 million to $1.2 billion.

Fast forward to 2014, and Wal-Mart has over $480 billion in sales and employs more than 2.2 million people that serve more than 200 million customers each week at more than 11,000 retail stores in 27 countries worldwide.

J.K. ROWLING

Joanne "J.K." Rowling was born in Yate, Gloucestershire, England. Her father was a Rolls-Royce aircraft engineer and her mother was a science technician. By the age of six, Joanne was writing fantasy stories and reading them aloud to her younger sister. She spent much of her teenage years depressed, due to her mother's deteriorating health and a strained relationship with her father. Having been rejected from attending Oxford University after high school, Joanne studied at the University of Exeter, where she received a Bachelor of Arts in French and Classics. After graduation, Joanne held jobs as a researcher and bilingual secretary for Amnesty International and the Manchester Chamber of Commerce.

At twenty-five years old, while waiting four hours during a train delay from Manchester to London, Joanne became inspired. In her mind, she could see so clearly a scrawny, black-haired, bespectacled boy who had no idea he was a wizard. She had never been this excited about an idea for a book before. Her mind flooded with details. Since she didn't have a pen to write, all she could do for the next few hours was think until she returned to her flat. That very night, she began writing *Harry Potter and the Philosopher's Stone*.

Not long after she began writing her novel, Joanne lost her mother after ten years of suffering from multiple sclerosis. This dramatically affected her writing. Depressed and wanting to escape from England, Joanne moved to Portugal to work as an English teacher at a language institute. Her new working hours allowed her to write during the day, while teaching in the afternoons and evenings. She married a Portuguese man and gave birth to a daughter, Jessica. The marriage didn't last. Joanne is said to have suffered from domestic abuse, even having to obtain a restraining order against her husband after he threw her out of their apartment one evening.

After Portugal, Joanne and her daughter moved to Edinburgh, Scotland, and lived on welfare. Jobless with a baby daughter to take care of, Joanne felt like a failure. She even contemplated suicide. Despite all of her struggles, she continued writing, often in cafes after her daughter fell asleep. After five years of writing, she typed her final manuscript on an old manual typewriter and sent the first three chapters to literary agents. After a number of rejections, one literary agent, Christopher Little, asked for the full manuscript after an enthusiastic reader on his team highly recommended her work. Little later agreed to become her agent.

Harry Potter and the Philosopher's Stone was originally submitted to twelve publishing houses, all of which rejected the manuscript. After a year of collecting dust, Joanne's manuscript was confirmed to be published by Bloomsbury, a publishing house in London, England. Barry Cunningham, an editor at Bloomsbury, gave the first chapter to his eight-year-old daughter, who loved it and asked to see the rest of it. Joanne was given an advance of £1,500 pounds from Bloomsbury, with a first printing of 500 copies. She was ecstatic. Joanne was going to become a published author, under the pen name J.K. Rowling, because Cunningham believed young boys did not like to read books written by women. Cunningham also advised Joanne to "get a day job, because there is very little chance of making money in children's books."

Joanne made an application to the Scottish Arts Council and received a generous grant of £8,000 pounds, which she used to focus on writing the next book in the series, *Harry Potter and the Chamber of Secrets*. Little then organized an auction for the American publishing rights of *Harry Potter and the Philosopher's Stone*. One bidder, executive director Arthur A. Levine of Scholastic Books, was highly enthusiastic about the book and won the auction, offering $105,000 for the rights. The book was published in the United States the following year, in 1998, and became a massive success, selling millions of copies worldwide.

J.K. Rowling has written seven books in the Harry Potter series, and, according to Guinness World Records, the series has sold over 400 million copies worldwide, with Joanne as the "first billion-dollar author" in history, having grossed over $1 billion from her novels and other related earnings.

STEPHEN KING

Stephen Edwin King was born in Portland, Maine. When he was two years old, his father left the family under the pretense of "going to buy a pack of cigarettes," but never returned. This left his mother, Nellie, all alone to raise Stephen and his older brother, David, under great financial strain. Nellie struggled to make ends meet for the family and often held two to three jobs at a time. Parts of Stephen's childhood were spent with his father's family in Fort Wayne, Indiana, in Stratford, Connecticut, and in Durham, Maine, where Nellie had taken care of her incapacitated parents.

From an early age, Stephen wanted to become a successful writer. He contributed articles to David's local newspaper, *David's Rag*. In high school, Stephen held a part-time job digging graves, which inspired him to write the short story, "I Was a Teenage Grave Robber," a tale about an orphan boy who accepts a job digging up bodies for a mad scientist. Although he was not paid, *College Review* accepted the short story. After all of the rejection letters Stephen had received thus far, he was finally in print.

After high school, Stephen enrolled at the University of Maine. He wrote every day and received his first check for $35 from *Startling Mystery Stories* for his short story, "The Glass Door," during his freshman year. As one of his professors put it, "We had many students who had aspired to become writers. What made Stephen different, from the beginning, was that not only did he aspire to become a writer, but he just went ahead and did it." He was active around campus in the antiwar movement and in student government, and starting from his sophomore year, Stephen wrote a weekly column for the student newspaper, *The Maine Campus.* However, writing was not earning him a living. To supplement the $5 per week his mother sent him, which Stephen later found out meant his mother would often live without eating, he took a job at the university library, where he met his wife, Tabitha Spruce.

The same year he graduated from the University of Maine with a Bachelor of Arts in English, Stephen was married and about to become a father. Living in a trailer park with his wife and daughter, and struggling to find work as a teacher, Stephen worked at a gas station for minimum wage and in a laundromat for $1.60 per hour. Tabitha worked nights at Dunkin' Donuts. Times were so hard that his family often had their phone disconnected, as they could not afford to pay their bills.

A year later, at twenty-four years old, Stephen found work as an English teacher at the Hampden Academy, a public high school, earning $4,600 per year. After their second child, Stephen took a job at the laundromat to supplement the income from his teaching job. After working all day, grading papers, and preparing lessons at home, Stephen retired to the trailer's furnace room to write for at least two hours each night. Earning around $200 per story, he developed an outlet for publishing stories via men's magazines.

Although Stephen was writing stories as fast as he could, his financial obligations mounted up. He vented his frustrations by smoking cigarettes and drinking alcohol at the local bar. He began writing a short story about Carrietta White, the daughter of an unstable religious fanatic, which he hoped to sell for a few hundred dollars to a magazine. However, Stephen felt he didn't know enough about teenage girls to be true to the character and threw his first draft in the trashcan. Tabitha found the draft, read it, and insisted he finish writing it. With his wife's help, Stephen finished *Carrie* (1974) in two weeks' time and sent it to an editor at Doubleday, who had previously accepted (and rejected) several of his manuscripts. The editor, pleased, asked him to make a few changes and resubmit his manuscript. Stephen did, and moved on with his writing and his life.

Then, one day at school, Stephen was called into the main office from the loudspeaker for a call from his wife. As he made his way to the office, Stephen's heart was beating rapidly. One of two things must've happened. Either something was wrong with one of his children, or he published his book. As they had their phone disconnected, Tabitha received a telegram from the editor at Doubleday stating they were going to publish *Carrie* and pay Stephen an advance of $2,500. Excited, Stephen and Tabitha spent the advance on a new car and moved into a small apartment.

Although life was better for his family, Stephen kept his day job of being an English teacher. He received a telephone call one day from the editor at Doubleday saying they sold the paperback rights for *Carrie* for $400,000. Stephen was entitled to half, meaning he was to receive $200,000, more money than he'd ever dreamed of. Upon hearing the news, Stephen dropped the phone and, as all of the strength had left his legs, slid down the wall behind him. Tabitha cried, and they embraced each other in their tiny apartment. *Carrie* sold over 1 million paperback copies within its first year and was also adapted into a major motion picture.

Stephen King has published more than fifty novels that have sold over 350 million copies worldwide. Many of his novels have also been adapted into feature films.

VIN DIESEL

Vin Diesel was born Mark Vincent in Manhattan, New York. He was raised in Westbeth, a tax-subsidized housing project for poor artists in Downtown Manhattan, by his mother, a retired astrologist, and his African-American stepfather, an acting instructor and theater manager. He has a younger brother and sister, as well as a fraternal twin, Paul. He never knew his biological father. At age seven, he and six other boys broke into an off-off Broadway house called the Theater for the New City near his home in Manhattan's Greenwich Village with the intent to vandalize it. When they were caught, Vin was scared, thinking Crystal Field, head of the resident drama company, would call the police. Instead, she offered him a job. He was handed a script and given a salary of $20 per week. From that point on, Vin wanted to become a successful actor.

By age fifteen, Vin was breakdancing for coins and lifting weights. He did not get much acting work growing up, so very little gave him self-gratification besides bodybuilding and women. "I told myself that if I'm not a movie star by eighteen, I'll quit and get a job. Then I said it again when I was twenty-one, and again at twenty-four: 'I won't be like these poor people chasing a dream of happiness that don't come true,'" Vin said. "I danced on street corners for money," he continued, "bought clothes and kept the tags attached so I could get cash back to pay rent. But during all the years I was broke, sleeping on someone's couch, I knew I'd be a movie star. No one else believed it, but I was going to break the mold."

Vin supported himself for nine years in New York City working as a bouncer. He changed his name to Vin Diesel while working at the popular nightclub Tunnel. Vin is short for Vincent and Diesel was the nickname given to him by his friends who said he ran off of diesel fuel, referring to his nonstop energy. At the same time, Vin was enrolled as an English major at Hunter College, but dropped out after three years to move to Los Angeles, California to further his acting career. He was twenty-four years old.

After two years of struggling to find acting work and even to find an agent, Vin returned to New York. His mother gave him the book *Feature Films at Used Car Prices* by Rick Schmidt, which ultimately showed Vin that he could take control of his career and make his own movies. Inspired, Vin created his own film, *Multi-Facial* (1995), a twenty-minute short about a racially-indeterminate actor who cannot land a job because of ethnic stereotyping, which he wrote in five days and filmed in less than three days with a budget of only $3,000. Later that year, *Multi-Facial* (1995) became a hit at the 1995 Cannes Film Festival, and people finally started to recognize Vin as an actor. The film was also noticed by filmmaker Steven Spielberg.

After the festival, Vin returned to Los Angeles and raised $50,000 through his telemarketing job of selling tools to fund the making of his first feature film, *Strays* (1997). He had written the manuscript for *Strays* (1997) prior to *Multi-Facial* (1995), but couldn't afford to film it at the time. As Vin once said, "So what successful people know and what I learned was, if you can't do it all, do what you can," explaining his reasoning for filming *Multi-Facial* (1995) prior to *Strays* (1997). To kick the film off the ground, Vin surrounded himself with a team of people who believed in him. He rehearsed with his fellow actors on the subway, in a way that everyone around them would think they were having a real conversation. Vin also encouraged the actors to shine with him in his scenes because doing so would only make the film stronger. Filming was a struggle. Vin had to fire the director of photography (DP) on the first day. After a week, he could no longer afford catering, so Vin made big pots of pasta and French bread for everyone. He also ran out of money at one point, and had to change the movie script to complete filming the following day.

Strays (1997) was accepted into the 1997 Sundance Film Festival, and although it received a good reputation, it didn't sell as well as he had hoped. Yet again, Vin returned to New York disappointed, only this time to receive a dream phone call. Steven Spielberg was impressed by *Multi-Facial* (1995) and wanted to meet Vin, eventually casting him in *Saving Private Ryan* (1998), starring Tom Hanks. The film was a huge success, grossing $481 million in the box office worldwide. *Multi-Facial* (1995) earned Vin even more work, when the director for *The Iron Giant* (1999) saw it and decided to cast Vin for the title role. Vin's acting career took off, and he starred in *Boiler Room* (2000), *Pitch Black* (2000), and the film that catapulted him into stardom, *The Fast and the Furious* (2001).

Arnold
Schwarzenegger

Arnold Alois Schwarzenegger was born and raised in Thal, Austria. His father was a police chief and his mother was a homemaker. Arnold grew up in a stone-and-brick building that had no plumbing, shower, or flushing toilet. Their water supply was a well they walked to a quarter of a mile away, so the family used as little water as possible. They all took showers using the same water, starting with his mother and father, followed by Arnold and his brother.

Growing up in a poor and strict household during the Cold War, Arnold, like most of the boys in his town, was often beaten by his father, who pulled his hair and whipped him with a belt, to serve as punishment for his wrongdoings. The discipline at school was no different from home, with the teachers hitting as hard as the parents. One of his friends was hit by a math teacher in the back of the head so hard that his face bounced on the desk, which broke his two front teeth. Hardships were routine, but Arnold never forgot how to withstand physical punishment.

Starting from an early age, Arnold had his eyes set on America. He believed he would go there one day. His vision was different from most childhood dreams. It was almost like a revelation to him. He told everyone about it: his parents, brother, friends, and even strangers on the street. "I'm going to America!" Arnold would often say. Although he didn't know how he was going to get there, he just knew he was going to do it. The people around him weren't convinced, but Arnold was, and he never stopped believing.

A history teacher assigned Arnold to an essay-writing assignment on Kurt Marnul, then-Mr. Austria, who had set a record in the bench press: 190 kilograms. Arnold was impressed by Marnul's achievement, but at the time, he didn't believe weightlifting had anything to do with him. During the summers, Arnold made friends with boxers, wrestlers, and other athletes at a popular summer hangout called Thalersee. He developed a close friendship with one of the lifeguards, Willi Richter, who was into weightlifting and brought Arnold along to train and to attend the World Weightlifting Championship with a few other guys in Vienna.

It wasn't until Arnold was fourteen years old when his vision became clearer. He wanted to become strong and muscular after watching the movie *Hercules and the Captive Women* (1961). Arnold was impressed with Hercules's body, portrayed by Reg Park, then-Mr. Universe. He also met Kurt Marnul, who was friends with Willi. Arnold was inspired when he saw Marnul's body, as well as all of the beautiful women who came with him. He wanted to be just like him. Arnold started training with Marnul, studying his entire workout schedule, as well as his techniques for pursuing women.

Although Arnold tried a lot of other sports, the gym totally consumed him. It was all he thought about. He even broke into a gym one Sunday when it was closed so he could train in the freezing cold. He had to wrap his hands in towels to prevent them from sticking to the metal bars. "Kurt Marnul can win Mr. Austria," he thought, "and he's already told me that I could too if I train hard, so that's what I'm going to do." Arnold's inspiration grew when he picked up a copy of *Muscle Builder* magazine and read the life story of Reg Park, growing up poor in England, to becoming Mr. Universe, to playing Hercules and living in "Muscle Beach," Santa Monica, California. He was sure that Park was a millionaire and always had beautiful women around him.

Suddenly, Arnold's dreams made sense. He refined his vision to become very specific. He was going to become another Reg Park. He was going to win the Mr. Universe title and break records in powerlifting. Then he was going to Hollywood, California. The vision had become so clear in his mind, it felt like it had to happen. There was no other alternative to him. It was this or nothing. This vision made all of the hours of lifting tons of steel and iron a joy. Every painful set and extra repetition pushed him one step closer toward his goal. Arnold became obsessed, even putting muscleman posters all over the wall behind his bed. With help from his friend, Arnold read muscle magazines by Joe Weider in English and converted an unheated section near the stairs into a home gym. He also won his first bodybuilding competition, in a beer hall, at fifteen-and-a-half years old.

While serving his mandatory one-year Austrian military commitment (required for all eighteen-year-olds) as a tank driver, Arnold went AWOL during basic training to compete in the Junior Mr. Europe contest. He won. Upon returning, however, Arnold was put in detention and spent twenty-four hours in a cell to serve as punishment. The competition meant so much to him, he didn't even think of the consequences. In the bodybuilding world, however, word spread of his victory. He was on the cover of several magazines and received several job offers as a personal trainer, including one from Rolf Putziger, who was Germany's biggest bodybuilder promoter. Excited, Arnold requested an early discharge, which was eventually approved.

Arnold made his way to Munich, Germany to work as a personal trainer for Rolf Putziger's gym. As the train approached the station, he overcame the questions in his head—"How will I find my way around? How will I survive?"—with his new mantra: "This is going to be my new home." He stayed at Putziger's apartment but left after a few days when Putziger bribed him, offering a car and a career in exchange for sex. Arnold moved into a storeroom at the gym, which he converted into sleeping quarters. He also split his daily workout routine into two sessions, two hours in the morning and two hours at night, to adjust to his busy schedule of training with clients.

Novices like Arnold usually competed for Mr. Austria and Mr. Europe, before competing for Mr. Universe. However, Arnold was impatient. He knew it could take years, and at the time, he wanted the toughest competition he could get. In a bold move, Arnold applied to compete in the Mr. Universe competition. Putziger, however, didn't want this to happen. He didn't want Arnold to get discovered and become successful before he could make money off of him. Jealous, Putziger destroyed his application in the mailroom and refused to pay for his trip to London, England. Thankfully, Arnold's friend Albert Busek persuaded the organizers to consider his new application, and Putziger's club rival, Reinhard Smolana, raised the money for Arnold's plane ticket.

Arnold placed second in his first Mr. Universe competition. Although he didn't win, he was in the spotlight. Magazines frequently mentioned him, and he was favored to win for next year. One of the judges, Charles "Wag" Bennett, was so impressed that he offered to develop a training program with Arnold for a few weeks. As Arnold had little money, Wag offered for him to stay in his crowded family home above one of his gyms in Forest Gate, London, England. Wag and his wife, Dianne, were like parents to Arnold, and even introduced him to his boyhood idol, Reg Park.

The training paid off. The following year, at age twenty, Arnold became the youngest to ever win the Mr. Universe title. Despite his success, Arnold knew that in order to fulfill his dream of going to America, he would have to dominate the European bodybuilding scene. One title was not going to cut it. He trained even harder for the next Mr. Universe competition. The day before, however, Putziger tried to coerce Arnold into signing an agency contract, which would entitle Putziger to a percentage of all of Arnold's future earnings, in exchange for Arnold's regular paycheck. Arnold was counting on this paycheck as spending money for his time in London during the competition. Arnold refused and left the gym with only the money in his pocket. He borrowed money from his friend Albert to pay for his plane ticket.

After Arnold won his second Mr. Universe title, Joe

Weider sent a telegram inviting Arnold to compete in the Mr. Universe competition in Miami, Florida, with all expenses paid. Arnold had finally arrived in America but placed second in the competition. Joe Weiner, however, agreed to cover Arnold's living expenses for a year so he could have another shot at the title. He believed in Arnold and wanted to document his journey via his bodybuilding magazine. At twenty-one years old, Arnold arrived in Los Angeles, California, without speaking much English. He enrolled in college, took English classes, and learned the American way of life. At Gold's Gym, Arnold trained as hard as ever and won multiple titles, including Mr. Olympia, which labeled him as the world's greatest bodybuilder. He also made his film debut portraying Hercules in *Hercules in New York* (1970) after Joe Weider convinced the movie producers to cast Arnold for the lead role.

Arnold became a prolific goal setter, writing his goals at the start of each year on index cards and succeeding in achieving them. He set out to achieve financial independence through a series of successful business ventures and investments. Inspired by fan mail he received asking for training advice, Arnold started a mail-order business, selling bodybuilding equipment and instructional tapes. He also started a brick-laying business with a fellow bodybuilder, which became successful due to the pair's marketing savvy and an increased demand following the 1971 San Fernando earthquake. Arnold reinvested the profits from both businesses and his competition winnings to purchase an apartment building.

After achieving massive success in bodybuilding, Arnold set out to achieve his goal of becoming a successful actor. It was difficult for him to find acting work in the beginning, as agents told him "that my body was 'too weird,' that I had a funny accent, and that my name was too long. You name it, and they told me I had to change it. Basically, everywhere I turned, I was told that I had no chance." However, Arnold was relentless. He starred in *Stay Hungry* (1976), which won him a Golden Globe for Best Acting Debut in a Motion Picture for his performance, and starred as himself in *Pumping Iron* (1977). His breakthrough films came starring as Conan in *Conan the Barbarian* (1982) and *Conan the Destroyer* (1984). He followed by starring as The Terminator in *The Terminator* (1984) under film director James Cameron, which catapulted Arnold into stardom.

JAMES CAMERON

James Cameron was born in Kapuskasing, Ontario, Canada. His father was an engineer at a power plant and his mother was an artist, nurse, and homemaker. James grew up in Chippawa, Ontario, and attended the Stamford Collegiate School in Niagara Falls, Ontario, before moving to Brea, California with his family when he was seventeen years old. From an early age, James was fascinated with movies, especially science fiction. In high school, he wrote many sci-fi stories. The dream of becoming a director, though, seemed unrealistic. He attended Fullerton College, a two-year community college, to study physics, which he later switched to English before dropping out, against his father's wishes. To make ends meet, James worked as a janitor, truck driver, machinist, and as a gas station attendant. At night, he often wrote and painted.

After watching *Star Wars* (1977) in theatres, James was inspired and quit his jobs, at twenty-four years old, to pursue his dream of being in the film industry. He taught himself special effects by reading books at his college's library. He wrote a ten-minute science fiction movie script with a couple of friends, entitled *Xenogenesis* (1978). They raised money, rented a camera, lenses, and studio, and filmed it. They dismantled the camera to understand how it operated and spent the first half-day of the shoot trying to get it running. James was the film's writer, director, producer, and production designer.

While educating himself on film-making techniques, James showed *Xenogenesis* (1978) to Chuck Comisky, then-head of special effects for New World Pictures (Roger Corman's independent film studio), who offered him a job on the spot as a miniature-model maker. Within three weeks, James had his own department. He developed a reputation as someone who got things done, as he often slept in the office because he worked so late. James also knew he had to create his own opportunities and asked Corman directly for promotions. Within a matter of weeks, James made his way from model maker to art director for the sci-fi movie *Battle Beyond the Stars* (1980). He also did special effects work design and direction on John Carpenter's *Escape from New York* (1981), production design on *Galaxy of Terror* (1981), and consultant work on the design of *Android* (1982). Making rapidly-produced, low-budget productions under Roger Corman taught James how to work efficiently and effectively.

James was hired as the special effects director for the sequel to *Piranha* (1978), entitled *Piranha II: The Spawning* (1981). However, after the original director for the film left due to creative differences, the film's producer gave James his first job as overall director. James didn't know, however, the producer was using American directors in order to secure funding from a small label at Warner Bros. As it turned out, the producer wanted the director's chair, whether it was official or not.

On location, production slowed due to numerous problems and adverse weather. James was fired as director just a couple of weeks into filming. The producer would not even allow James to review his own footage. James was told his shots weren't good, which bothered him more than getting fired. For the first time, James questioned his own talents. He questioned whether a career in film was right for him, all because of another man's opinion. Although he was fired, the producer kept James's name as director to secure funding. He knew James was broke and could not afford an attorney to have his name removed from the film. James flew to Rome a couple of months later to find out what really happened. The producer, once again, refused to show James his shots from the film. However, James found a way in and took a look at the film for himself. He realized his shots were fine and made just a few edits to the film before leaving.

While in Rome, James fell sick with a high fever and had a nightmare in his hotel room about a red-eyed, metal endoskeleton dragging itself out of a fire. He awoke inspired, drawing the robot he saw so vividly in his mind. At twenty-seven years old, James returned to Los Angeles and showed his sketches to Gale Anne Hurd, Corman's assistant, who became interested in the film. James enlisted his friend, Bill Wisher, to create an actual movie script.

After completing the screenplay for *The Terminator* (1984), James showed the script to his agent, who thought it was a lousy idea. In response, James fired him. He agreed to sell the production rights to Hurd for $1, with the promise that she only produce the film if James directed it. The two then shopped around the movie script. Although many of the production companies were interested, they were unwilling to let an inexperienced film director make the movie. One film distribution company, Orion Pictures, agreed to distribute the film if they could get the funding elsewhere. They eventually found a small production company, Hemdale Pictures, which was willing to let James direct.

James took a couple of writing jobs while waiting for Arnold Schwarzenegger to become available. James ultimately convinced Arnold to take the role as The Terminator after sending Arnold a painting depicting him as the human cyborg assassin. Hurd signed on as producer, and James finally got his first break as director. With a budget of $6.4 million, *The Terminator* (1984) was a smash hit at the box office, grossing $78 million worldwide. James became a major Hollywood director, with *Titanic* (1997) and *Avatar* (2009) as the two highest-grossing films of all time, at $2.19 billion and $2.78 billion respectively.

MARTHA STEWART

Martha Stewart was born Martha Kostyra in Jersey City, New Jersey. The second of six children, Martha grew up in a working-class community in Nutley, New Jersey. She started her modeling career at age thirteen, appearing in fashion shows as well as in television and print advertisements. A straight-A student, Martha achieved a partial scholarship to Barnard College, while modeling helped pay for expenses. After her sophomore year, she married Andrew Stewart, a law student.

Martha took a year off from Barnard after their wedding but returned to graduate with a double major in history and architectural history. After graduation, she continued her modeling career until her daughter Alexis was born in 1965. She started a second career as a stockbroker in 1967 for the boutique brokerage firm

Monness, Williams, and Sodel. When a recession hit Wall Street in 1973, Martha left the brokerage firm. She and Andrew moved to Westport, Connecticut, where they undertook the complete renovation of an 1805 farmhouse on Turkey Hill Road.

In 1976, Martha started a catering business, which she ran from the basement of her house. She also managed a gourmet food store in Westport called the Market Basket. Within ten years, Martha's basement business had grown into a $1 million enterprise, serving a number of corporate and celebrity clients. Catering publishers' parties in New York City led to a book deal. Martha Stewart's *Entertaining* was published in 1982 and became the best-selling cookbook since Julia Child's *The Art of French Cooking*, which was published twenty years prior. Martha continued to publish more books.

In addition to her books, Martha served as an editor and columnist for the magazine *House Beautiful*, as well as a contributing editor for *Family Circle*. While her career prospered, her personal life deteriorated. In 1989, Martha and Andrew Stewart divorced. In 1990, Martha started her own magazine, *Martha Stewart Living*, serving as editor-in-chief. The magazine became an immediate success. Appearances on *The Oprah Winfrey Show* and *Larry King Live* led to a regular weekly appearance on CBS's *Early Show*, as well as a series of holiday specials on the network. In 1993, she debuted a weekly half-hour television program, *Martha Stewart Living*, which eventually expanded to a daily hour-long broadcast with half-hour episodes on weekends.

Martha's television success transformed her into a household name. She launched a second magazine, *Martha Stewart Weddings*, in 1993. She also signed an advertising and consulting contract with retailer Kmart for a reported $5 million. In 1997, Martha purchased all of the publishing, broadcasting, merchandising and licensing ventures bearing her name and consolidated them into a new company, Martha Stewart Living Omnimedia. The company went public on the New York Stock Exchange (NYSE) on October 19, 1999.

JOHN GRISHAM

John Grisham was born in Jonesboro, Arkansas. The second eldest of five siblings, John's father was a construction worker and cotton farmer, and his mother was a homemaker. When he was four years old, John's family travelled around the South before settling in Southaven, DeSoto County, Mississippi. During his teenage years, John held a series of jobs, including mowing lawns, watering rose bushes at a nursery, laying chain-link fences, and working on a highway asphalt crew. He also worked as a "helper" for a plumbing contractor, where he crawled underneath houses, covered in sweat and mud, digging with a shovel until he discovered the problem. He often held his breath to the point of almost fainting. During his freshman year of college, John worked at Sears selling men's underwear, but quit when a corporate spy, posing as a customer, repeatedly caught him insulting customers.

For the first couple of years in college, John drifted. He thought about becoming a high-powered tax attorney, representing wealthy people who wanted to avoid paying taxes. He knew nothing about tax and did not know anyone who was wealthy. He ultimately attended three colleges before graduating with an accounting degree from Mississippi State University. He enrolled at the University of Mississippi School of Law to become a tax lawyer, until he took his first course in tax law. He was stunned by the complexity and barely passed the course. At the same time, John was involved in a few mock trial classes and realized he enjoyed practicing law in the courtroom. His plan of becoming a tax lawyer was discarded overnight, and John created a new career plan. He would return to his hometown, start his own firm, and become a hotshot trial attorney. As planned, John graduated from law school, with no job offers, and returned to his hometown.

At the time, there was no system for assigning a public defender in Southaven. For criminals, the judge appointed whatever attorneys happened to be in the courtroom that day. Essentially, the young attorneys took the low-paying cases after the more experienced attorneys got the better clients. John volunteered for all of the work he could get. He often felt bad for his clients, who were in trouble and depended on him, a rookie attorney. At the same time, while his law office was struggling, John ran for and won a House seat in the

Mississippi State Legislature. He was twenty-eight years old. His salary was $8,000 per year, which was a lot more than he had earned his first year of practicing law.

John spent the first three months of each year at the state capitol in Jackson, Mississippi, hearing court cases. Like most small-town lawyers, John was dreaming of the big case, the big verdict, the big trial where a law career is made. One day, he overheard the testimony of a twelve-year-old victim who had been beaten and raped. Her testimony was "gut-wrenching, graphic, heartbreaking, and riveting," according to John. Every juror was crying, and John remembers staring at the defendant wishing he had a gun. Suddenly, John became inspired. He never thought about writing professionally before, but a story formed in his mind over the following weeks. He thought of little else, but didn't know where to begin. At thirty-five years old, John took out his legal pad one evening and wrote Chapter One at the top, and the journey began.

John knew he had to write at least one page a day; otherwise, the book would go nowhere. He got into the habit of writing during early mornings, showing up at the office at 5:30 a.m. each day. As a result, people started talking about how hard he worked. Although he was doing sixty- to seventy-hour workweeks, his colleagues did not know he was also writing a novel. *A Time to Kill* was finished, from concept to finish, within three years. The book was rejected by twenty-eight publishers before

Wynwood Press, a then-unknown publisher, gave it a modest 5,000-copy printing. It didn't sell. Disappointed, as his dream to become a full-time writer was delayed, John convinced himself to write one more book. This time, he was going to write a book with a much broader appeal in a much faster time.

John remembered a friend of his, back in law school, who was a top student and heavily recruited by law firms in the area. He recalled speaking with his friend after one particular interview, who described the firm as the kind of place where once you join, it was almost as if you never leave, like it was owned by the Mafia. The idea stuck. John wrote the book in courtrooms, during early mornings, late in the office, whenever he had the chance to write. He titled it *The Firm*, a story about a hotshot young attorney who joins a law firm that showers him with money and gifts, which he later finds out is owned by the Mafia. He sent it to his agent, who shopped it around to book publishers. Nobody was interested.

Without John's knowing, someone in a copy room made a bootlegged copy of his manuscript and sold it, presumably to a talent scout. The talent scout then made his way around Hollywood, claiming to represent John, and shopped his manuscript around to the major movie production companies. Out of the blue, John received a call from his literary agent, who informed him they sold the movie rights for *The Firm* to Paramount Pictures for

$600,000. After the movie deal was complete, all of the major book publishing companies, which were initially not interested, fought over the publishing rights for his book. *The Firm* was published by Random House in 1991 and sold over 1.5 million copies in two years. It was also the best-selling book of 1991. After ten years of practicing law, at forty-one years old, John was finally able to quit his job and focus on writing full-time.

John Grisham has published twenty-nine novels that have sold over 275 million copies worldwide. Some of his novels include *A Painted House*, *The Runaway Jury*, *The Chamber*, *The Rainmaker*, *Skipping Christmas*, and *The Pelican Brief.*

SIR RICHARD BRANSON

Sir Richard Charles Nicholas Branson was born in Blackheath, London, England. The eldest of three children, Richard's father was a lawyer and his mother was a ballet dancer, flight attendant, and homemaker. Growing up, Richard performed poorly in school, being severely dyslexic, and could barely read by the age of eight. He developed an interest in sports and business from inheriting his mother's entrepreneurial spirit. At thirteen years old, Richard started his first business of growing Christmas trees. The business failed after rabbits ate most of the tiny sprigs.

At age sixteen, Richard started a national student magazine entitled *Student*. Working out of quarters in his school, Richard cold-called large corporations, including Coca-Cola and Barclays, trying to get them to advertise. He dropped out of school at age seventeen to focus full-time on the magazine, with his headmaster's departing words, "Congratulations, Branson. I predict that you will either go to prison or become a millionaire." He moved the magazine into the basement of his friend and business partner Jonny Gem's house, where they managed to land interviews with musical figures John Lennon and Mick Jagger. The first issue had a circulation of 30,000.

Student's offices moved to a commune, followed by the basement of a church, which was also known as "the crypt." Although the magazine grew in popularity, it wasn't making money. So Richard searched for ways to develop the *Student* brand in other directions. He thought about the high cost of records and the sort of people who bought *Student,* and wondered if he could advertise and sell cheap mail-order records through his magazine. He wanted to create a new name for the business, something that would be eye-catching, that could stand-alone and appeal to a broader audience. One of the girls on his team suggested the name Virgin, as they were all essentially virgins in business. The name stuck.

The orders poured in for Richard's new mail-order record service, which offered prices cheaper than its competitors. However, things took a turn for the worse after a postal strike that lasted six weeks delayed shipment of records. In response, Richard opened a record shop to sell records directly to consumers. Within a week, they found a location and opened Virgin Records, a record store with headphones and water pillows that catered to a younger generation of music lovers. It was as much a social hangout as it was a record store. Around the same time, Richard was also looking to create a recording studio that had a relaxed environment for recording artists, so he purchased a manor with fifteen bedrooms via a mortgage, his savings, and a loan from his aunt. By this point, the company's bank account was thousands of dollars overdrawn, and Richard was searching for ways to pay off his debt.

Richard devised and executed a plan where he illegally imported records and evaded paying a 33 percent record tax. While he was successful in paying off the debt in executing this plan, he was also arrested for tax evasion and spent the night in prison. His mother had to put up their home to bail him out. In order to avoid a criminal offense, Richard agreed to pay three times the illegal profit he had earned while conducting the scheme, to be paid over the next three years. If he failed to pay, he was to be rearrested and tried.

With a mortgage, overdrawn bank account, family loans, and now a hefty fine to pay off, Richard rolled the dice on some new business ventures. He, along with his team, opened thirteen more Virgin Records shops across the country and started their own record label, Virgin Music. With the current infrastructure in place, Richard could record, publish, promote, and distribute his artists' music. The first artist he signed was Mike Oldfield, who had originally failed to secure a record deal. Oldfield's debut album, *Tubular Bells* (1973), became a hit, selling millions of copies in Britain, and also became the soundtrack for *The Exorcist* (1973), which allowed the album to enjoy great success in the United States.

Richard reinvested all of the profits into growing the company and signing more artists, many of whom became commercial failures. The label initially struggled to sign big bands, including The Who, Pink Floyd, and The Rolling Stones. After repeated attempts, the label signed The Sex Pistols, whose debut album became a massive success and catapulted the label's image into the punk rock scene. Richard bought a private island in the Virgin Islands, and successful musical acts followed, including Human League, Culture Club, Simple Minds, and Phil Collins. With Virgin Music a success, Richard expanded his empire into megastores, film, books, and an airline service named Virgin Atlantic, which faced cutthroat competition from rival airline British Airways. The competition was so fierce that Richard had to sell Virgin Records in order to keep the airline afloat.

Virgin Atlantic became one of the United Kingdom's

largest airlines, and The Virgin Group is a multinational conglomerate that employs more than 50,000 people around the world, with over $24 billion in revenue (in 2012).

SYLVESTER STALLONE

Sylvester Gardenzio "Sly" Stallone was born in Manhattan, New York. His family moved to Washington, D.C., before settling in Philadelphia, Pennsylvania. Due to complications at birth, Sly was born with paralysis in some parts of his face, which resulted in a permanent slur of his speech. His father was a hairdresser and his mother was a dancer. His parents frequently fought and later divorced.

Growing up, Sly did not perform well in school. He was expelled three times. He also attended a special school for troubled children. After high school, Sly attended Miami State University to study drama, but dropped out and moved to New York to pursue an acting career. He always wanted to become an actor in movies to inspire people around the world to overcome their struggles, much like he was doing with his own life. To make ends meet, Sly worked all kinds of jobs, including cleaning lions' cages at the Central Park Zoo and ushering at a movie theater. Having been evicted from his apartment and homeless for several weeks, often sleeping in the Port Authority Bus Tunnel, Sly starred in the softcore pornographic film *A Party at Kiddy and Studs* (1970) for some money to get back on his feet.

At twenty-eight years old, Sly married Sasha Suzcuk and they moved into a small apartment building, which had no heating or air conditioning. He often fought with his wife, who wanted him to get a "real job." Sly was denied by many agents, who said they had no business for someone with an injured face. They went so far as to say that he was "dumb looking" and that he had no future in acting. However, Sly was persistent. He visited the same agents' offices five to ten times, repeatedly asking for acting work. In total, it is said he was kicked out of agents' offices an estimated 1,500 times. Sly eventually landed his first acting role after waiting overnight in one agent's office, who initially refused to see him. He proceeded to land minor acting roles, which never led to anything further.

While living in a cold apartment, Sly took comfort in the warm New York Public Library, where he discovered the poetry of Edgar Allen Poe. He also discovered his love for writing. Sly loved creating inspirational stories where the character overcomes an unbelievable situation, much like his own life. He wrote his own screenplays but had a tough time with selling them. He sold his first story, *Paradise Day*, for $100. Times were rough, and Sly had no money to feed himself, let alone his dog. On the lowest day of his life, Sly sold his dog for $25 to a man outside of a liquor store. Walking away from the sale, he cried, as he had lost his best friend.

A couple of weeks later, Sly watched the Muhammad Ali/Chuck Whepner fight on television. He watched as the underdog Chuck Whepner took Ali's punches and even managed to knock Ali out. Sly became inspired. The minute the fight ended, he started writing. He wrote for twenty straight hours. After three days, Sly completed writing a screenplay about a rags-to-riches American dream story of Rocky Balboa, an underdog boxer who overcomes his life's struggles as a club boxer and debt collector for a local loan shark to get a shot at the world heavyweight championship.

Sly pitched his movie script to agents around New York City. He received numerous rejections, with some agents labeling it as "predictable," "stupid," and "sappy," but Sly was relentless. One day, Sly met filmmakers Robert Chartoff and Irwin Winkler during an audition. Before he left, he mentioned that he was also a writer. The two filmmakers agreed to review Sly's screenplay and became interested after reading it. They offered to buy it from Sly for $360,000, under the condition that he not take the lead role. Sly refused. He was Rocky, and it was his script. He refused to let anyone else star in it, even though he was broke, starving, and barely making ends meet. After repeated attempts, the two filmmakers caved. They offered Sly $35,000 and the lead role in *Rocky* (1976) for the script. Sly gladly accepted. The first thing Sly did, after receiving the money, was return to the liquor store in hopes that the man he had sold his dog to would return. He did, and Sly purchased his dog back for $15,000 and a role in *Rocky* (1976).

With a budget of $1 million, *Rocky* (1976) was filmed in just twenty-eight days. Sly's body took a toll during the filming. At times, he almost collapsed on the floor due to physical exhaustion. To lower costs, he enlisted his family and close friends to play minor roles. His dog and its former owner were also cast into the film. *Rocky* (1976) was released on November 21, 1976 and became a sleeper hit, grossing $117 million in the box office nationwide. The film won Best Picture, Best Director, and Best Film Editing at the 1976 Academy Awards, with ten overall nominations, and catapulted Sly into stardom.

JACK MA

Ma Yun, also known as Jack Ma, was born in Hangzhou, Zhejiang Province, China. His parents were musician-storytellers. From the age of twelve, Jack had a strong desire to learn English. He would ride his bike for forty minutes, rain or snow, to a hotel near the city of Hangzhou's West Lake district, roughly 100 miles southwest of Shanghai. As China opened up, hordes of tourists stayed there, and Jack worked as a free tour guide to practice his English. Although he was not paid, he became more globalized than most Chinese people.

Jack failed the college entrance exam twice before being accepted by Hangzhou Teachers University, at twenty years old. He studied to become a high school English teacher and was active around campus, having been elected student chairman and, later, chairman of the city's Students Federation. He was the only graduate from his class to be offered a job as a teacher at a higher university (the others were placed in middle and high schools). His salary was approximately $12 to $15 per month. For five years, Jack taught English to college students and became famous locally as a dynamic and irresistible professor. He also taught night classes.

At age thirty, Jack rejected a promotion to become head of the college's external affairs department in order to start his own translation company, Haibo, which became known, in English, as the Hangzhou Hope Translation Company. He saw the need for translation, as his friends repeatedly asked for him to translate texts, and he hired retired professors to work for him. However, the company initially lost money, and Jack had to peddle goods on the street, including flowers, books, and clothes to earn a profit, all while still teaching.

As the company started to earn a profit, Jack was sent on a business trip to the United States, in 1995, by the Hangzhou municipal government. Jack became well-known for his ability to speak English, and the government authorized Jack to serve as a translator and mediator to collect the funds from an American investor who agreed to invest in a city highway project. During his trip, however, Jack discovered that the American investor was an international swindler. Jack was even lured to Las Vegas, Nevada by the swindler, where he won $600 from playing $25 at the slot machines in a casino.

Instead of going straight back to China, Jack used his casino winnings to take a flight to Seattle, Washington. Leaving his suitcase behind, Jack visited a small Internet service provider (ISP) named VBN. After searching for "beer" in one of the search engines and seeing there was no data involving China, Jack was inspired to create an Internet business in China. His idea was simple: pull together information on Chinese companies and publish them on a website, broadcasting their products to the entire world. His American friends at VBN would handle all of the technical aspects, with Jack handling all of the sales and promotion.

The same night Jack returned to Hangzhou, he invited twenty-four of his friends, all students of his at night school (who also worked in foreign trade), to a meeting in his apartment. He spoke for two hours on his vision. In the end, only one person agreed to go into business with Jack. He started China Yellow Pages, and raised over $2,000 from his family to start the company. At the time, he knew nothing about computers or telecoms. He worked day and night in selling webpages to local Chinese businesses. As there was no direct access to the Internet in China, Jack had to translate the text and send all of the images to be developed by the workers at VBN in Seattle.

As the Internet developed in China, Jack noticed a lot more competition entering the marketplace, many of

THRIVE: 30 INSPIRATIONAL RAGS-TO-RICHES STORIES

whom were American-educated, Chinese-born Internet entrepreneurs who raised capital in the United States. In 1996, after a year of competing, the general manager of Hangzhou Telecom proposed a joint venture agreement with Jack, offering $167,000 in exchange for 70 percent of China Yellow Pages. Jack accepted. However, Jack also resigned just months later, as Hangzhou Telecom now controlled his company and was looking to grow and make money quickly, while Jack was looking to grow the company slowly and carefully. After his departure, from 1998 to 1999, Jack headed an information technology (IT) company established by the China International Electronic Commerce Company (CIECC), which resulted in the first ministerial-level website in China.

It was Jack's dream to run his own e-commerce company. His intuition was telling him that the high tide of the Internet was coming fast, and he would miss it if he were to stay in government. So, in 1999, Jack called together all of the members of his team and said, "First, you can go work with Yahoo! I'll recommend you and I know that the company will not only welcome you but the salaries will be high. Second, you can work for Sina or Sohu: they'll similarly welcome you and the salaries won't be too bad. Or third, you can come home with me. However, you'll get just $95 in salary per month, you'll have to rent your own flat and live within a five-mile radius of where I live, since in order to save money I won't allow you to take taxis, and moreover you'll have to work in my home. You make your decision." He gave them three days to decide. Everyone filed out of the room. Within three minutes, everyone returned. They all chose to be with Jack.

Jack and his team of eighteen then travelled south, from Beijing to Hangzhou. He asked everyone to invest their own money, without borrowing from friends or family, to start the company. In total, they raised $60,000. Then Jack made a speech: "We aim to create an e-commerce company, and in doing this we have three specific goals. First, we want to set up a company that lasts for one hundred and two years. Second, we want to establish a company that provides e-commerce services to China's small- and medium-sized companies. Third, we want to set up the world's largest e-commerce company, one that will enter the ranks of the top ten names among global Internet sites." The company's name would be Alibaba. Jack wanted a name that would be recognizable at a global level. He purchased the domain name, Alibaba.com, from its owner in Canada for $10,000.

During the preparatory stage for Alibaba, Jack and his team worked day and night in his apartment, often sixteen to eighteen hours each day. Alibaba was officially launched in March 1999. Jack attracted free media attention using what he had learned setting up China Yellow Pages and the time he spent fraternizing with journalists in Beijing, China. By the end of 1999, however, money was running low. The company attracted international media attention after *BusinessWeek* wrote about a seller offering AK-47s via Alibaba's platform. Although the article negatively affected the company to a degree, it also attracted venture capitalists. Piles of investment offers lined up. However, Jack turned down many offers, millions of dollars' worth of potential investment, before accepting a $5 million investment from Goldman Sachs in October 1999. The following year, in October 2000, the company completed an additional $25 million round of investment. Alibaba continued to grow over the years, having survived the crash of the dot-com bubble (2000-2002), as well as the SARS outbreak (2002-2004) in China.

In October 2014, Alibaba Group Holding Ltd. went public on the New York Stock Exchange (NYSE) and raised $25 billion, marking it as the largest IPO in history. Alibaba is also one of the largest e-commerce platforms in the world.

OPRAH WINFREY

Orpah "Oprah" Gail Winfrey was born in Kosciusko, Mississippi. Her mother, an unmarried teenager at the time of Oprah's birth, was a housemaid and her father was a coal miner turned barber turned city councilman. Oprah spent the first six years of her life in rural poverty with her maternal grandmother. Her family was so poor that Oprah wore dresses made of potato sacks, which the local children often teased her for. Her grandmother taught her how to read and write by age five, so Oprah quickly moved to the first grade.

From the age of nine, Oprah was molested by her cousin, uncle, and a family friend. At thirteen years old, after suffering years of abuse, Oprah ran away from home. When she was fourteen, she became pregnant, but her son was born prematurely and died shortly after birth. Oprah attended Lincoln High School, but after success in the Upward Bound program, she transferred to the affluent suburban Nicolet High School. There, her poverty was rubbed in her face as she rode the bus to school with fellow African-Americans, some of whom were servants of her classmates' families. To keep up with her free-spending peers, Oprah stole money from her mother and dated older boys. Her mother then sent Oprah to live with her father in Tennessee.

Despite her struggles at home, Oprah became an honors student, was voted Most Popular Girl, and joined her high school speech team at East Nashville High School, placing second in the nation for dramatic interpretation. At age seventeen, Oprah won the Miss Black Tennessee beauty pageant. She also attracted the attention of the local African-American radio station, WVOL, which hired her to do the news part time. She worked there during her senior year of high school and during her first two years of college. She also won an oratory contest, which secured her a full scholarship to Tennessee State University, where she majored in speech communication and performing arts.

After graduating from college, Oprah worked in local media as both the youngest news anchor and the first African-American female news anchor on Nashville's WLAC-TV. She later moved to Baltimore's WJZ-TV to co-anchor the six o'clock news. However, she was removed after only seven months because the producers thought she was too "dull" and "stiff." Instead of firing her, they had her co-host a failing early-morning talk show called *People Are Talking*. She also hosted the local version of *Dialing for Dollars*.

Oprah relocated to Chicago, Illinois to host WLS-TV's low-rated, half-hour morning talk show, *AM Chicago*. Within months of taking over, the show went from last place in ratings to overtaking *Donahue* as the highest-rated talk show in Chicago. Movie critic Roger Egbert persuaded Oprah to sign a syndication deal with King World. The show was renamed *The Oprah Winfrey Show*, expanded to a full hour, and broadcasted nationally on September 8, 1986.

The Oprah Winfrey Show remained the number one talk show for twenty-four consecutive seasons and received forty-seven Emmy awards, until Oprah stopped submitting the show for consideration in 2000. She launched her own American television channel, The Oprah Winfrey Network, on January 1, 2011.

AL PACINO

Alfonso "Al" Pacino was born in Manhattan, New York. His father was an insurance salesman and his mother was a homemaker. He was raised by his grandparents and his mother after his parents divorced when he was two years old. Al was a shy kid growing up in the South Bronx, New York. He developed an interest in acting while performing in school plays. At age seventeen, Al dropped out of school and left home, holding a variety of jobs to support himself, including work as a messenger, busboy, janitor, movie usher, mover, shoe salesman, superintendent, and as a postal clerk.

Al was often unemployed and homeless, sleeping on the street, in theaters, and at friends' houses. He acted in basement plays and was originally rejected to be a member of the Actors' Studio, a prestigious membership association of professional actors, theatre directors, and playwrights. Instead, he enrolled in the Herbert Berghof Studio (HB Studio) and learned under acting teacher Charles Laughton, who became his mentor and best friend. At the age of twenty-two, Al lost his mother due to anemia. His grandfather passed away the following year. Al sunk into a deep depression and began abusing alcohol, while seldom eating or sleeping. He even collapsed on the street, one morning, while delivering newspapers.

Al took whatever acting jobs he could get, including stand-up comedy and children's theatre. After four years in the HB Studio, Al was accepted into the Actors Studio, and under the guidance of acting coach Lee Strasberg, Al successfully launched his career. He was finally able to focus on acting full-time and develop a stronger confidence for his craft. He began acting in plays, making it big with *The Indian Wants the Bronx* (1968) and *It's Called the Sugar Plum* (1968), for which Al won an Obie Award. Film producer and personal manager Martin Bregman saw the play one night and signed on to become Al's manager. Al made his Broadway debut starring in Don Petersen's *Does a Tiger Wear a Necktie?* (1969), which received rave reviews and a Tony Award.

Following his success in theatre, Al received many offers to star in movies but turned down eleven before he made his big screen debut. After a brief appearance in *Me,*

Natalie (1969), an independent film starring Patty Duke, Al starred in *The Panic in Needle Park* (1971), portraying a sensitive junkie. He was thirty years old. He used his own personal experiences with alcohol abuse for the film. During filming, he was noticed by film director Francis Ford Coppola, who was impressed with Al's performance. At the time, Coppola was developing *The Godfather* (1972) and was convinced that Al's brooding intensity would be perfect for the film.

Not everyone, however, shared Coppola's vision. Al improvised his way through his two auditions, convinced he didn't stand a chance. The studio was heavily against him taking the role. In the end, Coppola was successful for fulfilling his overall vision for the film. Al took the role and became an international celebrity overnight, winning an Oscar nomination for Best Supporting Actor for his performance as Michael Corleone in *The Godfather* (1972).

JON HAMM

Jonathan Daniel "Jon" Hamm was born in St. Louis, Missouri. His father ran a family trucking company and his mother was a secretary. His parents divorced when he was two years old. Jon's mother died of colon cancer when he was ten years old, so he moved in with his grandmother and father. He started acting at an early age, with his first performance as Winnie the Pooh in the first grade.

In high school, Jon was both a drama kid and a jock, playing Judas in *Godspell* and a middle linebacker on the football team. After graduation, and after turning down several athletic scholarships, Jon attended the University of Texas to study English. However, he dropped out after his father died, due to diabetes and general poor health. He moved back home and lived in the basement of his older half-sister Julie's house, where he fell into a deep depression. At twenty years old, Jon had lost both of his parents. Fighting suicidal thoughts and prescribed Prozac for a month, Jon recovered and graduated from the University of Missouri on a drama scholarship, where he performed in fifteen plays in just two years. After graduation, Jon taught eighth grade acting for some time, as a gesture of repayment for the school's support during his adolescent years.

At twenty-four years old, Jon headed for California with $150 and his Toyota Corolla to pursue an acting career. He moved into a house with four other aspiring actors and took a job as a waiter while attending auditions. Finding acting work was tough for Jon, primarily due to his older appearance. He once said, "If you didn't look eighteen years old, you weren't working. And I didn't look eighteen years old when I was eighteen. I always looked ten years older than I was."

After three years of not landing a single acting role and after being dropped from his agency, Jon took a job as a set dresser on a softcore pornographic film, earning $150 per day. He then made himself a promise. He would give himself five more years. Five years, and if his acting career wasn't going by the time he was thirty years old, he was in the wrong field. At that moment, his entire life changed, and it was like he started working right away. Jon found career-making work portraying a fireman on the drama series *Providence*. His one-episode contract grew to nineteen, and Jon was finally able to quit waiting tables and pursue acting full-time. He landed minor roles in Clint Eastwood's space adventure *Space Cowboys* (2000), independent comedy *Kissing Jessica Stein* (2001) and *We Were Soldiers* (2002), having turned thirty years old during filming. His career was further bolstered by minor roles in television series, including the recurring role of police inspector Nate Basso on Lifetime's *The Division.*

Jon auditioned, along with more than eighty candidates, for the protagonist character Don Draper in AMC's television series *Mad Men.* He went through numerous auditions, each time explaining to the casting directors that he had a lot of personal experience to offer, as both Jon and Draper were not raised by parents. Jon also used memories of his father, who was very similar, to portray Draper. He was at the very bottom of everyone's list, but creator Matthew Weiner believed in Jon and fought for him to win the role. He did, and *Mad Men* premiered on July 19, 2007 with over 1.4 million viewers, catapulting Jon into stardom.

JERRY SEINFELD

Jerome Allen "Jerry" Seinfeld was born in Brooklyn, New York. His father was a sign maker and his mother was a homemaker. From the age of eight, Jerry dreamed of becoming a successful comedian. He was heavily influenced by his father's comedy, as well as the comedy of television comics, including Abbott and Costello and Bill Cosby. Jerry worked tirelessly on his comedy routines throughout middle and high school. After high school, Jerry attended Oswego College in upstate New York, but later transferred to Queens College in New York City.

Shortly after graduating from college, Jerry performed stand-up comedy for the first time. It was a disaster. Terrified, Jerry could only mumble a few ineffectual words into the microphone. Although he had failed, Jerry was eager to try again. He wrote a new act and appeared at different comedy clubs. He landed the position of emcee at The Comic Strip and observed the comedians as they performed. He was a hard worker with a strong attention to detail. He also refused to use profanity in his stand-up routines.

Jerry worked for many years as a freelance comedian at different clubs. At twenty-six years old, Jerry headed for Los Angeles, California to join its growing comedy club circuit. After a year, he landed a small role on the television series *Benson*, where he went from earning $40/night in the clubs to $4,000/episode. Although Jerry thought he was good, the producers thought otherwise. He arrived at rehearsals one day to discover there wasn't a script for him. After just three episodes, Jerry was fired, in a rather humiliating way.

Devastated, Jerry returned to stand-up in the comedy clubs. One night, a producer saw his act and booked him to be on *The Tonight Show with Johnny Carson*. To prepare for the show, for thirty days, Jerry ran five miles and practiced his comedy routine during the same five minutes he would perform. He wanted to be sure there was no chance he would fail at this opportunity. All of the hard work paid off, as Jerry became a hit on the show and was asked back several times.

Following his success on television, Jerry went on a comedy tour around the United States, performing over 300 shows per year. He was driven, and his dreams seemed to be just within his grasp. However, things took a stumbling turn when Jerry's father died of cancer. Jerry stopped touring and found it difficult to move on. His father had a huge impact on his life, and now he was gone.

It took six weeks before Jerry was able to return to the comedy stage. Not long after, an executive from NBC approached Jerry and offered for him to create his own television special. The only problem, however, was Jerry had no idea what the show should be about. His friend and fellow comedian, Larry David, helped Jerry with creating the pilot, entitled *The Seinfeld Chronicles*. The pilot almost failed to go on the air, as the show was generally negatively received by test audiences. NBC originally passed on the show, but NBC executive Rick Ludwin convinced his superiors and even offered his own personal budget to order four more episodes, which is considered to be the smallest order for a sitcom ever received on a network. The four episodes aired a year later, and *Seinfeld* became one of the most successful sitcoms in television history, with nine seasons and 180 episodes. The series finale, "The Finale," aired on May 14, 1998 with 76.3 million viewers.

TONY ROBBINS

Anthony "Tony" Robbins was born Anthony J. Mahavorick in North Hollywood, California. His father was a parking garage attendant and his mother was a homemaker. The eldest of three children, Tony's birth parents divorced when he was seven, and his mother remarried twice. One husband, Jim Robbins, a semi-professional baseball player, adopted Tony. At Glendora High School, Tony excelled in his studies and was elected student body president during his senior year. Despite his academic success, his home life was chaotic and abusive. On Christmas Eve, when Tony was seventeen, his mother chased him out of the house with a knife. Tony left and never returned.

Tony stayed at a friend's house, trying to figure out what to do with his life. He called his uncle, who owned a cleaning business, and asked him for a job. Working as a janitor on late nights, Tony rode the bus to and from work and often did not sleep until 3:00 a.m. Following the advisement of his high school guidance counselor, who said he had enough credits to graduate, Tony left school to concentrate on supporting himself. His mother insisted that his uncle fire Tony, so he could learn how to support himself on his own, not using family. Tony agreed.

Tony took a sales job, which he found in the local newspaper, selling music club subscriptions door to door. He proved to be a good salesman, and in just a few months after leaving high school, Tony earned enough money to move into his own apartment. While making a sales pitch to a new customer, he learned about self-help guru Jim Rohn. The customer took great interest in Tony and informed him about one of Rohn's upcoming seminars. Tony attended, and at the end of the seminar, he approached Rohn and asked him for a job. Rohn gave him one, and Tony promoted Rohn's seminars to businesses all over Los Angeles, California, earning over $3,000/month.

After graduating from high school, Tony immersed himself into his new career. He kept a journal and read as many books on psychology and personal development as he could. He was eventually promoted to having his own office and earned over $10,000/month. However, as his career was taking off, Tony's personal life deteriorated.

He had broken up with his girlfriend and his friends grew jealous of his success. Tony was stunned, as his success was making him lonelier than ever. He started sabotaging himself by not showing up to sales meetings and eating excessively. He gained thirty-eight pounds and his business was failing. At twenty-one years old, he moved into an apartment on Venice Beach, California, where he spent most of his days watching soap operas.

One day, Tony forced himself out of his apartment and began jogging along the beach. Staring out at the waves, he decided to take back control of his life. Tony turned his life around and began conducting his own seminars at a friend's house in Vancouver, Canada. He ended his seminars with a firewalking exercise in his friend's backyard. The exercise proved that, using their minds, anyone can overcome their fears, including walking on fire. Tony grew his reputation as a self-help guru through a series of radio guest appearances, and he eventually moved his seminars back to California. He achieved mainstream success through infomercials promoting his products and through his bestselling books, *Unlimited Power* (1987) and *Awaken the Giant Within* (1991).

SHANIA TWAIN

Shania Twain was born Eileen Regina Edwards in Windsor, Ontario, Canada. Her biological parents divorced when she was two years old, and her mother, Sharon, moved to Timmins, Ontario, taking Shania and her two younger sisters with her. Sharon then married Jerry Twain, a Native American, and the couple had a son together, Mark. Jerry adopted Shania and her sisters, legally changing their last names to Twain.

From the age of three, Shania showed an interest in music. By age ten, she was writing her own songs. Her mother fully supported her music career. Despite their financial struggles, her mother spent every extra dollar on developing Shania's talents, including paying for vocal lessons in Toronto, Ontario. She also took Shania around to perform at local bars and on television programs. As her father was in and out of work and refused government handouts, Shania and her siblings were often starving. Her parents also frequently fought, with her father often physically abusive toward her mother. At age sixteen, Shania joined a cover band called Flirt that travelled all around Ontario.

At age twenty-one, Shania's parents were fatally killed in a car accident, leaving Shania in charge of her three younger siblings. Devastated, Shania moved to Huntsville, Ontario. Under the advisement of a family friend, she took a job singing at a local resort. She moved the family into a house with no electricity or running water, where they bathed and washed their clothes in the nearby river. Shania performed every night and managed to pay the rent and provide for her younger siblings. After nearly four years, Shania's siblings were older and moved out on their own, and Shania was ready to advance her musical career. She assembled a demo tape, and her manager set up a showcase for her to present to record executives. Within a few months, she was signed to Mercury Nashville Records.

Shania recorded and released her debut album, *Shania Twain* (1993), which sold an unimpressive 100,000 copies. After failing to receive radio airplay, Shania turned to television and released a series of music videos. Her videos were noticed by Sean Penn and producer Robert "Mutt" Lange, who both wanted to work with her. With Lange, Shania recorded and released *The Woman in Me* (1995), which has sold over 12 million copies in the United States and became the best-selling country album by a female artist in history. She followed with *Come On Over* (1997), which has sold over 17 million copies in the United States, breaking the record she had previously broken.

HARRISON FORD

Harrison Ford was born in Chicago, Illinois. His father was an advertising executive and actor, and his mother was an actress and homemaker. Growing up, Harrison was often bullied in school. He was an intelligent student but didn't apply himself, which resulted in a steady C average. After high school, Harrison attended Wisconsin's Ripen College, where he was a member of a college fraternity. In the summers, Harrison held various jobs, including work as a tree trimmer, floral delivery boy, and chef aboard private yachts. He initially did not know how to cook, but taught himself on the job via books and newspaper columns.

Realizing he would never be able to use a philosophy degree, Harrison became discouraged with his academic studies and spent much of his senior year eating pizza and sleeping. Due to his poor attendance and low test scores, Harrison was informed he would not graduate just three days prior to the graduation ceremony. Harrison returned to his hometown with student loans and no degree. College did one thing for Harrison, though. During the final semester of his senior year, he enrolled in a drama class and overcame his fear of speaking in front of a live audience. As his friends graduated and accepted office jobs, Harrison pursued an acting career because he believed it would provide him with opportunities to confront new and interesting challenges in life.

Harrison started acting in a handful of productions at a local theater. The first few productions helped Harrison completely overcome his fear of public speaking, as well as develop his love for acting. He performed in plays at the Belfry Theater in Wisconsin with his then-girlfriend, Mary. The night before their debut performance, the couple wed in a small ceremony at a local church. After acting for months in consecutive nightly performances, Harrison and his wife set out for Los Angeles, California to make the transition from the acting stage to the movie screen.

When he arrived in Los Angeles, Harrison found work as a salesman for a local paint supply store, as a rigger aboard a yacht, and as a late-night pizza maker in Hollywood. He also performed in local plays and was recognized by the media. One onlooker was a Hollywood composer who insisted Harrison meet with a studio executive at Columbia Pictures. Harrison attended the interview, and after being asked questions about his height, weight, and foreign language skills, he was shown the door. Disappointed, Harrison made his way through the corridors toward the elevators. Before the elevator arrived, he was ecstatically approached by one of his interviewers, who requested he return to the room.

Harrison signed a seven-year contract with Columbia Pictures to work as a contract player. He was paid a weekly salary and attended acting classes, eventually making his debut appearance as a bellboy in the film *Dead Heat on a Merry-Go-Round* (1966). He was in the movie for just under one minute, which did not even qualify him to be in the closing credits. Before its release, the studio's vice president called Harrison into his office after reviewing a copy of the film. He criticized Harrison's performance and suggested acting was a waste of his time and efforts. Harrison argued with the vice president and was ultimately punished with an additional six months of training.

Harrison was cast in a few more films while at Columbia Pictures. However, his contract was terminated after just eighteen months. He was let go in a rather unpleasant way. Here is part of his conversation with the producer in charge of his contract: "I don't think you're worth a thing to us. But I know your wife is pregnant, you need the money, so I'll give you another couple of weeks. Just sign the paper my secretary has. Okay, boy? Now, get out of here." After arguing with the producer, Harrison was abruptly terminated from his contract. Three days later, however, he signed a similar contract with Universal Studios.

Harrison was looking for his big break to propel himself out of auditions and minor acting roles and into the lifestyle of a successful actor. However, Harrison was a father with a family to take care of. He accepted a number of roles, those he would never have accepted, on and off the big screen (including work as a cameraman) to support his family. By the age of twenty-eight, Harrison had two sons and a home that required many repairs, which he had chosen to fix himself. He studied carpentry books at the local public library and became skillful, to the point that he sold his carpentry skills to supplement his acting income.

Within a few years, Harrison developed a reputation as being the "carpenter to the stars." His first well-publicized job was for Brazilian composer-producer Sergio Mendes. Spending $100,000, Mendes hired Harrison to convert his three-car garage into a recording studio. He was recommended by a friend, and did an exceptional job. Although he was excelling with his carpentry business, Harrison never gave up on his dream of becoming a successful actor. It was because of carpentry that Harrison was able to be more selective with the acting roles he accepted.

After passing on a number of roles over the next few years, one script from film director George Lucas, who hired Harrison to build cabinets in his home, captured his full attention. To take the role for *American Graffiti* (1973), Harrison took a 50 percent pay cut (comparing to his carpentry business). With just a $750,000 budget, the movie grossed over $115 million at the box office nationwide and put Harrison into the spotlight. Lucas later hired Harrison to read lines for actors auditioning for parts in *Star Wars* (1977). Harrison's talent had surfaced, and he was cast to star as Hans Solo. *Star Wars* (1977) became one of the most successful films of all time, grossing over $775 million in the box office worldwide, and catapulted Harrison into stardom.

TYLER PERRY

Tyler Perry was born Emmitt Perry, Jr. in New Orleans, Louisiana. His stepfather was a carpenter and his mother was a preschool teacher. He was raised in an abusive household in New Orleans, where his father beat him often. Tyler was beaten so hard one time that he blacked out for three days. By age ten, Tyler had been molested by three men and by one of his mother's friends. He later discovered that his father molested one of his friends, as well. To escape from his external surroundings, Tyler used the power of his imagination. Even when his father was screaming at him at the top of his lungs, Tyler just closed his eyes to a peaceful mind and visualized himself living and being in a much better and freer place, often playing in a park that his mother and aunt had taken him to.

One day, Tyler became inspired by a comment made on

The Oprah Winfrey Show on how writing about difficult experiences could lead to personal breakthroughs. Inspired, Tyler wrote a series of letters to himself that became the basis for his first musical. In a giant leap of faith, at twenty-one years old, Tyler headed to Atlanta, Georgia, in a Hyundai Excel that leaked so much transmission fluid, he had to stop every two hours to siphon more fluid back into the engine. He managed to save $12,000 from working various jobs as a car salesman and bill collector to invest into his first play, *I Know I've Been Changed*. He rented a 1,200 person theater in Atlanta, certain he'd end the night with $20,000 in his pocket from ticket sales. He didn't. Only thirty people showed up, mostly friends and colleagues he'd invited to come see the play. Within a week, Tyler was broke and homeless, living in seedy motels and in his car.

For six years, Tyler peddled the play through church appearances. He managed to save enough money to keep the play going, working as a construction worker and car salesman. Then, one day, Tyler decided to quit. He was tired of all of the rejections and heartbreaks. He was tired of having his play performed in front of an empty theater. Fortunately, his friends pushed him to do one more show at Atlanta's House of Blues, which a promoter booked for a limited run. Tyler agreed, and right before the show, he called and forgave his father for all of his misdoings. The show was a hit and performed in front of a sold-out crowd. "Maybe I visited the right churches," Tyler said.

"Maybe I finally got the word out. But until I die, I'll believe that when I finally forgave my father, the Lord blessed the play."

According to *Forbes*, by 2005, Tyler had generated "more than $100 million in ticket sales, $30 million in videos of his shows, and an estimated $20 million in merchandise," and "the 300 live shows he produces each year are attended by an average of 35,000 people a week." He successfully transitioned to filmmaking with his breakthrough film, *Diary of a Mad Black Woman* (2005), which grossed $50 million in the box office nationwide. He opened his own film production studio, Tyler Perry Studios, in 2006.

HENRY FORD

enry Ford was born and raised on a farm in Greenfield Township, Michigan. From an early age, Henry was fascinated with machinery. He saw his first automobile, a self-powered steam engine, at twelve years old with his father on their way to Detroit, Michigan, just a few months after his mother passed away during childbirth. Henry immediately saw the potential of what a "horseless carriage" could have on people's lives, especially farmers. By age thirteen, he was disassembling and reassembling timepieces, and often fixed the timepieces of friends and neighbors.

Henry's father expected him to eventually take over the family farm, but Henry despised farm work. He wanted to pursue a career in machinery. At age sixteen, Henry left the family farm for Detroit and found work as a machinist, where he operated and serviced steam engines. He eventually abandoned the idea of a steam-powered automobile, after deeming it too dangerous, and searched for an alternative. He also studied bookkeeping and worked nights at a local jewelry store repairing watches. After three years, Henry returned to the family farm, while working occasional stints at Detroit factories. He married Clara Bryant, who had grown up on a nearby farm. In the first several years of their marriage, Henry supported his new family by running a sawmill.

Henry eventually returned to Detroit with his wife and found work at Thomas Edison's Edison Illuminating Company, where he was promoted to chief engineer within two years. On call twenty-four hours a day, Henry spent irregular hours working on his side efforts to build a gasoline-powered horseless carriage, which he completed in 1896 and named the Ford Quadricycle. That year, Henry also attended a meeting with executives and was introduced to Thomas Edison. Encouraged by Edison, Henry designed and built a second vehicle, which he completed in 1898. Backed by the capital of Detroit lumber baron William H. Murphy, Henry resigned from the Edison Illuminating Company and founded the Detroit Automobile Company. However, the automobiles produced were of a lower quality and higher price than Henry wanted. After many disagreements with his business partners, Henry left the company, which was renamed the Cadillac Motor Car Company.

A year later, Henry formed the Ford Motor Company with $28,000 in capital. He released a new car every few months, beginning with the Model A and making his way through the alphabet. The Model T was introduced in October 1908 and became a tremendous success. The car was simple to drive and cheap to repair. The price of the car dropped over the years, and people who had never thought they would own a car before, including farmers, were now driving Henry's invention. By 1918, half of all cars driven in the United States were Model Ts. At forty-five years old, Henry's dream had finally come true.

CHARLIZE THERON

Charlize Theron was born in Benoni, Transvaal Province, South Africa. Her biological parents were co-owners of a road construction company. At age six, Charlize started attending ballet lessons, and at age twelve, she was sent to a boarding school to study dance. Her home life, however, grew strained. Her father fell into alcoholism and physically abused her mother. One weekend, while Charlize was home from camp, her father assaulted her mother, who in turn shot him dead. The incident was viewed as self-defense, and her mother did not serve any prison time.

At age sixteen, Charlize entered a Johannesburg modeling contest and won. She flew to Italy to represent South Africa at the International New Model Today competition. She won again, and attended modeling gigs all over Europe. A year later, Charlize moved to New

York City to study at the Joffrey Ballet School and supported herself attending modeling gigs. However, she was forced into early retirement after injuring her knee in class.

Charlize then travelled to Los Angeles, California to pursue an acting career. However, she found her Afrikaner accent a barrier in landing speaking roles. In turn, Charlize watched hours of television to improve her dialect in order to hide her South African roots. It was 1994, and Charlize was broke, living in a cheap hotel and eating primarily bread she had taken from restaurants. During an argument with a bank teller, who refused to cash a $500 check from her mother's South African bank account, Charlize was discovered by John Crosby, a long-time talent manager. Crosby organized acting classes, and within months, Charlize made her acting debut in *Children of the Corn III: Urban Harvest* (1995). She then landed roles in *2 Days in the Valley* (1996) and *That Thing You Do!* (1996).

By 1997, Charlize established a reputation as one of the most promising actresses in Hollywood, appearing in *Trial and Error* (1997), a few television series, as well as in an advertisement for Martini. She entered mainstream Hollywood starring alongside Keanu Reeves and Al Pacino in *The Devil's Advocate* (1997).

ELLEN DEGENERES

Ellen DeGeneres was born and raised in Metairie, Louisiana. Her mother was a speech therapist and her father was an insurance salesman. From an early age, Ellen developed an interest in comedy. At age thirteen, when her parents divorced, Ellen had used her comedy in order to make her mother laugh. She attended King High School but graduated from Atlanta High School when her mother remarried and moved to Atlanta, Louisiana, bringing sixteen-year-old Ellen with her.

Ellen attended the University of New Orleans but dropped out after one semester. She then held a series of jobs, including work as a secretary at a law firm, selling vacuum cleaners, waiting tables, painting, a hostess, and as a bartender. She fell in love with her roommate, Kat Perkoff, and the two moved into a house together. With Kat's support, Ellen wrote short, humorous essays she hoped would be published in magazines. She loved to make people laugh, and her peers took notice. A friend invited her to perform at a luncheon she was hosting. Ellen performed with no written act, eating a hamburger and French fries. She was a hit, and friends encouraged Ellen to write an act and perform stand-up comedy. She did, and became instantly addicted to the local comedy scene.

Ellen's personal life deteriorated when she discovered Kat was cheating on her. Ellen moved out, hoping to teach Kat a lesson. A few days later, she ran into Kat at a comedy club but pretended not to hear her. Later that night, Kat was killed in a car accident. Ellen had driven past the accident but didn't realize it was her until the following morning. To overcome this devastating event, Ellen engaged in a monologue to God in her head, questioning why he could possibly let this happen. The monologue eventually developed into a stand-up routine called Phone Call to God, which Ellen became convinced she would perform on *The Tonight Show with Johnny Carson* someday. She became the emcee at Clyde's Comedy Club in New Orleans, Louisiana and performed at small venues across the country. Ellen sent a video of her stand-up routine to compete for television network Showtime's Funniest Person in Louisiana competition and won. She followed by winning Showtime's Funniest Person in America competition at twenty-seven years old.

Despite winning the competition, Ellen continued to perform in small venues with often tough audiences. Then, one night, Ellen performed her Phone Call to God routine with an associate producer for *The Tonight Show with Johnny Carson* in the crowd. Impressed, the associate producer booked Ellen to perform on the show, just as she had envisioned. She was a hit, and became the only female comic to be invited by Carson to the famed couch after her performance. After the show, Ellen received multiple offers to perform stand-up at comedy clubs.

Ellen then made her way into television, having landed a small role on the television series *Open House*. However, the show was cancelled after one season. She then took on another supporting role on the television series *Laurie Hill*, which was also cancelled after a few episodes. However, the show's creators, Neal Marlens and Carol Black, were impressed with Ellen and created a television show around her, titled *These Friends of Mine*. The show struggled during its first season and was renamed *Ellen*.

Ellen reached its height in popularity when Ellen publicly came out as a lesbian on *The Oprah Winfrey Show* in February 1997. She also announced her character's homosexuality on *Ellen*, which attracted major media attention, as well as 46 million viewers for the airing of "The Puppy Episode" on April 30, 1997. The bold move shaped Ellen into an outspoken advocate for gay rights.

However, ABC cancelled the show after pressure from religious rights groups.

With her career spiraling down, Ellen took on small movie projects and returned to stand-up comedy. She received wide exposure after hosting the 2001 Emmy Awards. After repeated attempts, she landed another television sitcom, *The Ellen Show*, which was cancelled after just one season due to poor ratings. She followed by launching a daytime television talk show, *The Ellen DeGeneres Show*, later renamed *Ellen,* which aired on September 8, 2003 and proved to be a critical hit and commercial success. On March 12, 2013, NBC renewed the show through the 2016-2017 television season, marking over thirteen seasons on television.

DAVID NEELEMAN

David Neeleman was born in Sao Paulo, Brazil. His father was a journalist, as well as the Latin American bureau chief for the United Press International (UPI), and his mother was his father's assistant before becoming his wife. The second son and child of seven children, David and his family moved to Utah when David was five years old. Growing up, David performed poorly in school, and was nearly held back in the third grade. He was later diagnosed with adult attention-deficit disorder (ADD) in his early adulthood. Toward the end of high school, David couldn't read or write well, not even managing to read a whole book.

David enrolled at the University of Utah but left after his freshman year to serve his church as a missionary for two years in Brazil. Preaching the Mormon religion, David developed his salesmanship and leadership abilities. By the end of his mission, he had baptized over two hundred converts. When he returned to the United States, he re-enrolled at the University of Utah and married his college sweetheart, Vicki Vranes. They had their first child together the following year.

David had no idea what he wanted to do with his life. However, during his sophomore year, he spotted a business opportunity from a classmate in an accounting class. The classmate had a connection in Hawaii who was having trouble selling timeshares. Intrigued, David called the connection and engineered a deal where they both could make money. David agreed to pay $125 per week, whenever a timeshare was not rented. In turn, David advertised the timeshares available in the local newspaper and collected over $500 in sales for each one, generating a few hundred dollars profit. Eventually, David made three to four of these deals every day.

As demand increased, David negotiated for more rooms to rent and packaged his deals with charter flights to Hawaii. His business expanded, and David built a full-fledged travel agency, making over $100,000/year in his early twenties. By his junior year of college, annual sales at his travel agency were over $8 million, and he had twenty-one employees. Against the advisement of his parents, David dropped out of college to focus on his growing debt-free business.

Things took a turn for the worse when The Hawaii

Express, the charter airline David used to package the deals, became financially unstable. The airline was losing money and had to cut its already-low fares to compete against the other major airlines. The Hawaii Express eventually filed for bankruptcy, which ended David's travel agency as well. He lost $500,000 of his clients' money after the hotels refused to issue refunds. With his dreams lost, David's company filed for bankruptcy, and he left the travel industry. At twenty-three years old, David was jobless with his wife and two children to support.

Although his first business failed, David built a good reputation for himself in the travel industry. June Morris, head of Morris Travel, a $50 million agency with one hundred employees, became aware of David's creativity and sales skills. After learning from David's uncle, who was her accountant, about the bankruptcy, she called David to recruit him for her travel agency. David initially refused to answer her phone calls. He was planning on entering the drapery business and wanted nothing to do with the travel industry anymore. However, Morris ultimately prevailed in persuading David to work at her travel agency.

It did not take long before David rekindled his interest in the travel industry. Within a short period of time, David became a key employee at Morris Travel. He negotiated higher commissions from hotels and airlines, and brought in a lot of new business for the growing travel agency. He always had plenty of ideas to go around, which he gives thanks, in large, to the ADD he learned to embrace as a gift (and refused to take medication for). One such idea of his was for a discount airline service. David cofounded Morris Air with June Morris in 1984, initially offering cheap flights from Salt Lake City, Utah to Los Angeles, California. David introduced many game changing ideas to the industry, including ticketless travel and an inexpensive, online call reservation system that employed work-at-home mothers. The company was a tremendous success and was sold to Southwestern Airlines for $129 million in 1994, making David a wealthy man at thirty-four years old.

After the acquisition, David worked for Southwestern Airlines under then-CEO Herb Kelleher. Although the two had a mutual respect for one another, David was fired after just five months. David cried when he was given the news. As he had signed a non-compete agreement that was effective for five years, David served as CEO of OpenSkies, a touch screen airline reservation and check-in systems company, which was acquired by HP in 1999. He also cofounded WestJet, another upstart airline he built into Canada's second largest airline within five years.

As his non-compete agreement inched toward expiration, David planned his next big idea, a discount airline based in New York that delivered the best service. Pulling in nearly $120 million from investors, David formed his new airline, JetBlue, in 1999, with operations beginning in 2000. The upstart airline offered cheap flights with a luxury service, including leather seating, more legroom, and live satellite television. Combined with clever marketing, the airline became a massive success, being consecutively rated the nation's #1 airline year after year. However, things took an unexpected turn on Valentine's Day 2007 when New York City was hit with a major ice storm. Most of the airlines cancelled their flights. David, however, sent his planes to the runway, thinking the storm would pass. It didn't. As a result, customers were stuck on the tarmac and at the airport for hours. Consequently, David was ousted as CEO. It was the lowest point of his career, as he put his heart and soul into JetBlue.

David was never one to quit. This time, he raised $225 million to start an airline service in Brazil. Azul, which means "blue" in Portuguese, offers flights that are cheaper and faster than taking buses throughout the growing country. According to the National Civil Aviation Agency of Brazil (ANAC), in March 2013, Azul had 17 percent of the domestic market share in terms of passengers per kilometer flown.

MARK CUBAN

Mark Cuban was born and raised in a middle-class neighborhood in Pittsburgh, Pennsylvania. His father worked at a car upholstery shop and his mother was a homemaker. His grandfather emigrated from Russia and supported his family by selling merchandise out of the back of a truck. At age twelve, Mark sold garbage bags door to door in order to save for a pair of shoes. Throughout high school, he worked as a stamp and coin salesman.

Mark skipped his senior year of high school to enroll at the University of Pittsburgh, before transferring to Indiana University a year later. To earn a profit, Mark taught disco classes, started a chain letter, and raised $15,000 from one of his college professors to open a bar. It was popular around campus but was forced to close because of a wet T-shirt contest involving an underage girl. After graduation, Mark moved back to Pittsburgh and took a job with Mellon Bank, which was looking to install computers. Mark immersed himself in the study of machines and networking, while working to incorporate an entrepreneurial spirit into his job. He often wrote notes to the CEO, invited senior executives to happy hour to network with the younger employees, and started a newsletter. His boss, however, felt threatened. "Who the f— do you think you are?" he yelled.

At twenty-four years old, Mark quit his job and travelled to Dallas, Texas in his 1977 Fiat X19 that had a hole in the floorboard and needed oil every sixty miles. He moved into a tiny apartment with five friends and slept on the floor. Mark had no closet or dresser, so he stacked his clothes in a corner. He worked as a bartender, while applying for other jobs. He interviewed with a company named Your Business Software, which sold PC software to businesses and consumers, one of the first in Texas. At the time, Mark bought a $99 Texas Instruments computer and taught himself how to program in code. The company was impressed and offered Mark a sales position at $18,000 per year, plus commission. Mark accepted.

Nine months into his job, Mark was about to close a $15,000 sale for the company. However, he was fired for closing the sale instead of opening the store that morning. This was the turning point of his career. Mark went back to the customer and asked him for the job with his newly-formed company, MicroSolutions, which sold software, provided training and configured computers. The customer agreed. Mark eventually expanded his company into selling local-area networks, installing personal computers (PCs) for small- and medium-sized businesses, as well as reselling products from Televideo and Novell. MicroSolutions grew into a company with $30 million in revenues, which Mark later sold to CompuServe in 1990 for $6 million. He later invested profits from the sale to start AudioNet, later renamed Broadcast.com, which Mark wisely sold to Yahoo, in 1999, at the height of the dot-com bubble for $5.7 billion in stock. The sale made Mark a billionaire.

JAY Z

Shawn Corey "Jay Z" Carter was born and raised in Brooklyn, New York. His father left the family when he was eleven years old, so Shawn was raised by a single mother in the drug-infested Marcy Houses, a housing project in Brooklyn's Bedford-Stuyvesant neighborhood. The youngest of four children, Shawn expressed an interest in rapping at an early age, often waking his siblings late at night, banging drum patterns on the kitchen table. To make ends meet, Shawn sold drugs during the American crack epidemic. At age twelve, Shawn shot his brother in the shoulder for stealing his jewelry.

Shawn turned to rap to escape from the drugs, violence, and poverty that surrounded him in the projects. While honing his rapping skills, Shawn also participated in local freestyle battles and accompanied his mentor and local rapper, Jaz-O, in recording a song called "The Originators," which won the pair an appearance on an episode of *Yo! MTV Raps*. He also changed his rap name from "Jazzy" to "Jay-Z." The project ultimately became a commercial failure. Disappointed, Shawn dropped out of high school and resumed selling drugs. Although he was still rapping, he was also struggling to secure a record deal, even after touring with successful American rapper Big Daddy Kane in 1994.

At twenty-four years old, Shawn met his business partner Damon "Dame" Dash, and the two started working together, releasing Shawn's first single, "In My Lifetime" (1994), via a singles-only record deal with Payday Records. In 1995, after determining they could market records better themselves, Shawn and Dame opened their own record label, Roc-A-Fella Records, with the intent of recording and distributing Shawn's first independent album. They took on a silent partner, Kareem Burke, to fund the project. The label also landed a distribution deal with Priority Records and rented a cheap office in Manhattan, New York on John Street.

After the success of Shawn's second single, "Ain't No Nigga" (1996), which later became part of *The Nutty Professor* (1996) soundtrack, the label released Shawn's debut album, *Reasonable Doubt* (1996). The duo sold Shawn's album throughout New York City from the backs of their cars. By the end of 1996, the album sold over 420,000 copies. Shawn also raised a higher profile for himself due to his appearance on The Notorious B.I.G.'s posthumous *Life after Death* (1997). Shawn followed with releasing *In My Lifetime, Vol. 1* (1997), and the album that launched him into stardom, *Vol. 2... Hard Knock Life* (1998), which has sold over 5.4 million copies in the United States.

URSULA BURNS

U rsula Burns was born in Manhattan, New York. She was raised by a single mother in the Baruch Houses, a rough public housing project on the Lower East Side of Manhattan. Although she grew up poor, Ursula's mother often told her, "Where I was didn't define who I was." Her mother also spent nearly half of her annual salary on Catholic high school tuition for Ursula and her two siblings. In school, she was prepared for one of three career options: nun, teacher, or nurse. However, none of these careers interested Ursula.

As her mother insisted on a college education, Ursula attended the Brooklyn Polytechnic Institute with the intent of studying chemical engineering, which she learned about from a Barron's book at the New York Public Library. She later switched majors and graduated with a Bachelor of Science in Mechanical Engineering.

She was accepted into an educational program that offered to pay for her master's degree at Columbia University, as well as offered a summer mechanical engineering internship at Xerox Corporation.

Ursula started her career at Xerox as an engineer working in a research lab. After nearly three years, Ursula was approached by a human resources employee who taught her about the company's products and services. She held various roles in product development and planning throughout her 20s. In 1990, Ursula's career took an unexpected turn when Wayland Hicks, a senior executive, hired Ursula as his executive assistant. The following year, she became executive assistant to chairman and chief executive officer Paul Allaire. From 1992 to 2000, Ursula led several business teams, including the company's color business and office network printing business.

In 2000, Ursula was named senior vice president, Corporate Strategic Services, heading up manufacturing and supply chain operations. Alongside chief executive officer Anne Mulcahy, Ursula restructured Xerox through its turnaround to emerge as a leader in color technology and document services. In April 2007, Ursula was named president of Xerox, expanding her leadership to also include the company's IT organization, corporate strategy, human resources, corporate marketing, and global accounts. She was also elected a member of the company's board of directors. Ursula was named chief executive officer in July 2009, making her the first African-American woman to head a Fortune 500 company. She became chairman of Xerox in 2010, leading the more than 140,000 employees of Xerox who serve clients in more than 180 countries.

JOHN D. ROCKEFELLER, SR.

John Davidson Rockefeller, Sr. was born in Richford, New York. His father was a travelling salesman and con artist, commonly known by the locals as "Big Bill" or "Devil Bill," who identified himself as a botanic physician and sold elixirs to his victims. His mother was a homemaker and devout Baptist who struggled to create a sense of stability in the household, largely due to Bill's extended traveling and philandering. John's family moved frequently throughout New York before settling in Strongsville, Cleveland, Ohio.

The second eldest of six children and the eldest son, John did his share of household chores, including raising turkeys, selling potatoes and candy, and lending sums of money to neighbors. Bill instilled in John and his siblings, whenever he was around, to think big and to always get the better part of any deal. His father once bragged, "I cheat my boys every chance I get. I want to make 'em sharp." John developed a sense of frugality from his mother, who often purchased goods via a credit line at the local store, due to Bill's extended travelling. John was also advised by his pastor to make as much money as he could, so he could contribute to his church and to charities.

At sixteen years old, John searched for his first real job in Cleveland. Always neatly dressed in a dark suit and black tie, John visited the same businesses three times before landing an assistant bookkeeper position with Hewlett & Tuttle, commission merchants and produce shippers. John immersed himself in the position, working long hours and learning all of the methods and systems of the office. He impressed his employers with his seriousness and diligence. He went to great lengths to collect overdue accounts. Although he was not well-paid for this job, whatever money he earned, John gave to his church and to local charities.

At twenty years old, John set out on his own. After raising $4,000 from investors, John started a produce commission business, Clark & Rockefeller, with his business partner and neighbor, Maurice Clark. In 1860, at the end of their first year in business, the company grossed $450,000, with a profit of $4,400. The following year, the company earned $17,000 in profit. John heavily borrowed money from banks to expand the business. However, John realized that the commission market business in Cleveland was going to be limited. He became convinced that railroads would be the primary transportation for agricultural commodities. He also believed the future of Cleveland would lay in the collection and shipment of raw industrial materials, not agricultural commodities.

On August 27, 1859, Edwin Drake struck oil near Titusville, Pennsylvania, which started a frenzied oil boom. Although the technology Drake used was not new, the idea of pumping oil out of the ground, like with water, was. John investigated the feasibility of entering the oil refining business in 1862, and the firm Andrews, Clark & Company was formed in 1863. John believed the key to success was a strong attention to detail and ironing out all of the inefficiencies for every business. At twenty-four years old, John bought out the Clark Brothers share for $72,500 and gained complete control over the business. He heavily borrowed money from the banks and invested all of the profits back into the business to expand his empire.

In 1866, John brought his brother, William Rockefeller, into the business, and they built another refinery in Cleveland named Standard Works. They opened a New York City office, with William in charge of the company's exporting business. In 1867, Henry M. Flager, whom John worked with in the commission market business, was added to the partnership, and Rockefeller, Andrews & Flager was formed. Flager's wife's uncle became a silent partner and made substantial investments into the partnership.

John realized that the only way to make money consistently was to make the business as large as possible and to fully utilize all of its waste products. He cut efficiencies down to the smallest detail. The partnership built high-quality refineries using the best materials and owned their own cooperage (barrel-making) plant, which cut the cost of a barrel from $3.00 to less than $1.50. The partnership also owned tanks, warehouses, boats, and their own drayage service to transport their oil. On January 10, 1870, The Standard Oil Company of Ohio was formed by John D. Rockefeller (30%), William Rockefeller (13.34%), Henry Flagler (16.67%), Samuel Andrews (16.67%), Stephen Harkness (13.34%), and O. B. Jennings (brother-in-law of William Rockefeller) (10%). At the time of its formation, the company held a 10 percent market share in the oil business and expanded by acquisition. By 1872, the company had quietly absorbed most of the oil refineries in Cleveland. The company also built its own pipeline system to more cheaply and efficiently distribute their oil.

In response to state laws limiting the scale of companies,

John and his associates created innovative ways to manage their fast-growing enterprise. On January 2, 1882, they combined their disparate companies, spread across dozens of states, under a single group of trustees, entitled The Standard Oil Trust. By 1904, the trust had installed a nationwide distribution system that served 80 percent of all American homes and businesses. At its peak, John's company held a 90 percent market share of the oil industry. The Standard Oil Trust was eventually dissolved in 1911, under the Sherman Antitrust Act, and split into thirty-four individual, independent companies. ExxonMobil, Chevron, ARCO, Marathon Petroleum, and Imperial Oil are all direct descendants.

John D. Rockefeller, Sr. is widely considered to have been the richest man in history. Until his death in 1937, John's assets equaled 1.5 percent of America's total economic output, the equivalent of $340 billion today.

HOWARD SCHULTZ

Howard Schultz was born in Brooklyn, New York. He was raised in a poor household in the Bayview Houses in Canarsie, Brooklyn. When he was seven years old, Howard's father broke his ankle and was out of work for several weeks. His mother, who was seven months pregnant at the time, couldn't work either. So his family had no income, no health insurance, no worker's compensation, and nothing to fall back on. Howard answered the telephone at night, with specific instructions from his mother, to inform bill collectors his parents weren't at home. The family borrowed to make ends meet until his father was able to return to work.

After high school, Howard attended Northern Michigan University on a football scholarship, where he received a Bachelor of Science in Communication. He was the first person from his family to graduate from college. After graduation, Howard didn't know what he wanted to do with his life. He stayed in Michigan and found work at a nearby ski lodge. After a year, he returned to New York and got a job with Xerox Corporation in their sales training program. His training included six months of cold calling, as well as knocking on office doors in midtown Manhattan to gather prospects. He became a good salesman, and earned good commissions for three years. He paid off his college loans and even rented an apartment in Greenwich Village, Manhattan, with a roommate. He met his wife, Sheri Kerish, one summer in the Hamptons.

Although he was doing well, Howard wanted a more challenging career. A friend of his had mentioned that a Swedish company, Perstorp, was planning on setting up a U.S. division for its Hammarplast housewares subsidiary. Howard thought this was a great opportunity to get in on the ground floor of a growing company. The company initially placed Howard in a division selling building supplies. They moved him to North Carolina, where he sold components for kitchen and cabinet furniture. However, Howard hated what he was selling. After ten months, he threatened to quit. To prevent him from leaving, Perstorp transferred Howard to New York and promoted him to vice president and general manager of Hammarplast. He was given a salary of $75,000, as well as a company car, an expense account, and unlimited travel, which included trips to Sweden four times a year. He was also selling products he liked.

By age twenty-eight, Howard and Sheri had rewarding careers and were living in Manhattan's Upper East Side, where they owned an apartment. One day, Howard noticed a small retailer in Seattle, Washington that was placing unusually large orders for a certain type of drip coffeemaker. Starbucks Coffee, Tea, and Spice had only four small stores then, yet it was buying this product in quantities larger than Macy's. Curious, Howard flew to Seattle to investigate. Founded in 1971 by three partners (two teachers and a writer) as a single store near Seattle's famed Pike Street Market, Starbucks sold freshly roasted gourmet coffee beans as well as teas, spices, and various coffee-making accessories. The company enthralled Howard. By the time he left Seattle to return to New York, Howard was determined that Starbucks was his future.

It took Howard a year, however, to convince the original owners of Starbucks to hire him. He flew to Seattle often, arriving prepared with a list of ideas for Starbucks to share with the owners. He repeatedly sold himself as to what skills and experience he could offer to the company. However, after "interviewing" him one evening over dinner, the owners initially rejected him. They thought it was too great of a risk to hire a "high-powered New Yorker," and they were afraid he would steer the company in the wrong direction, away from their vision. After hearing the news, Howard did not give up. He convinced one of the owners over the phone to reconsider. The following morning, Howard got the job and agreed to take a steep pay cut for a small equity share, giving up his luxurious lifestyle and prestigious job in the process. Everyone, including his mother, thought he was crazy.

Howard and Sheri then prepared to drive across the country to their new home in Seattle. Shortly before they left, Howard learned his father had lung cancer and was expected to live for only a year. He went to the hospital to say goodbye to his father, as he was not sure when he would be able to see him again. "Go to Seattle," his dad said. "You and Sheri have a new life to start there. We can handle things here." Howard and Sheri proceeded with moving to Seattle, with a cloud of worry hanging above them. During his early months at Starbucks, Howard worked behind the counter greeting customers, as well as tasting the different kinds of coffee. After a year, the company sent him to Milan, Italy to attend an international housewares show, where Howard discovered the country's love for coffee bars. He became convinced that this was the future for Starbucks, as well as for the American way of life. He returned to Seattle and shared what he discovered. However, the owners weren't interested. To them, Starbucks was a retailer, not a restaurant or bar.

Over the months, Howard grew weary. He was convinced that coffee bars were the future. So he left Starbucks to start his own coffee company, Il Giornale, with $400,000 in seed capital, $150,000 of which came from Starbucks. He immediately followed with raising a $1.25 million round of investment. Over the course of a year that he spent raising the money, Howard spoke to 242 people, with 217 saying no. Many of the investors he approached had bluntly told him he was selling a crazy idea. One of them even said, "Why on earth do you think this is going to work? Americans are never going to spend a dollar and a half on coffee." He heard all of the arguments as to why coffee was not going to become a growing industry, but he never let them stop him. He raised the money and opened three more stores.

Two years after starting Il Giornale, Howard came across an opportunity to buy Starbucks, as the owners were looking to cash out and concentrate on their other business, Peet's Coffee & Tea, which they had acquired a few years earlier. Howard raised $3.8 million to acquire Starbucks in 1987. He merged the two companies, named it Starbucks, and started to expand. At the time of its initial public offering (IPO) in June 1992, Starbucks had 140 stores with $73.5 million in revenue. Fast forward to 2014, and Starbucks has 21,878 stores and $14.89 billion in revenue (in 2013).

SOURCES

Jim Carrey

"Ace Ventura: Pet Detective (1994)." *Box Office Mojo.* IMDb.com, Inc., n.d. Web. 6 Feb. 2015.

"Jim Carrey." *IMDb.* IMDb.com, Inc., n.d. Web. 6 Feb. 2015.

"Jim Carrey." *Jim Carrey.* Web. 7 Feb. 2015.

Leeds, Sarene. "Jim Carrey Talks About 'SNL' Audition Disaster on 'Letterman'." *Speakeasy.* The Wall Street Journal, 30 Oct. 2014. Web. 6 Feb. 2015.

OWN TV. "What Oprah Learned from Jim Carrey | Oprah's Lifeclass | Oprah Winfrey Network." Online video clip. *YouTube.* YouTube, LLC, 13 Oct. 2011. Web. 6 Feb. 2015.

"Season 16, Episode 110." *Larry King Live*. CNN. 19 Dec. 1999. Television.

Eminem

Baker, Ernest, David Drake, Insanul Ahmed, and Lauren Nostro. "The 25 Biggest First-Week Album Sales in Music History." *Complex*. Complex Media Inc., 27 Mar. 2013. Web. 7 Feb. 2015.

"Eminem." *Bio.com*. A&E Television Networks, n.d. Web. 6 Feb. 2015.

"Eminem." *Biography*. A&E Television Networks. 2009. Television.

"Eminem Album Sales Statistics." *Statistic Brain*. Statistic Brain Research Institute, n.d. Web. 6 Feb. 2015.

"Eminem | Biography." *AllMusic*. AllMusic, n.d. Web. 6 Feb. 2015.

Kreps, Daniel. "Eminem and The Beatles: The Top-Selling Artists of the 2000s." *Rolling Stone*. Rolling Stone, 9 Dec. 2009. Web. 7 Feb. 2015.

LaChapelle, David. "Eminem Blows Up." *Rolling Stone*. Rolling Stone, 29 Apr. 1999. Web. 6 Feb. 2015.

Sam Walton

Hayes, Thomas C. "Sam Walton Is Dead At 74; the

Founder Of Wal-Mart Stores." *The New York Times.* The New York Times Company, 5 Apr. 1992. Web. 7 Feb. 2015.

"History Timeline." Wal-Mart Stores, Inc., n.d. Web. 3 Feb. 2015.

Walton, Sam, and John Huey. *Sam Walton, Made in America: My Story.* New York: Doubleday, 1992. Print.

J.K. Rowling

"First billion-dollar author." *Guinness World Records.* Guinness World Records, n.d. Web. 7 Feb. 2015.

"Harry Potter and Me." *Biography.* A&E Television Networks. 21 Jan. 2002. Television.

"J.K. Rowling." *J.K. Rowling.* Web. 7 Feb. 2015.

Kleffel, Rick. "Harry Potter and the Pot of Gold." *Metroactive Books.* Metro Publishing Inc., n.d. Web. 7 Feb. 2015.

Miller, Chloe. "JK Rowling On Getting Published." Urbanette Magazine, n.d. Web. 7 Feb. 2015.

"The JK Rowling Story." *The Scotsman.* Johnston Publishing Ltd., 16 June 2003. Web. 7 Feb. 2015.

Watson, Julie, and Tomas Kellner. "J.K. Rowling And The Billion-Dollar Empire." *Forbes.com.* Forbes.com LLC, 26 Feb. 2004. Web. 07 Feb. 2015.

Stephen King

"About the Author." *StephenKing.com*. Stephen King, n.d. Web. 2 Feb. 2015.

King, Stephen. *On Writing: A Memoir of the Craft*. New York: Scribner, 2000. Print.

Olmsted, Larry. "New Horror Film Festival & Stephen King's Upcoming 'Shining' Sequel." *Forbes.com*. Forbes.com LLC, 4 Apr. 2013. Web. 7 Feb. 2015.

"Stephen King: Fear, Fame and Fortune." *Biography*. A&E Television Networks. 17 Jan. 2000. Television.

Vin Diesel

"An Interview with Vin Diesel." *Film4*. Film4.com, n.d. Web. 7 Feb. 2015.

Raider, Dotson. "The 'Misfit' Who Made Good." *Parade*. 26 Feb. 2006: 16-18. Print.

"Saving Private Ryan (1998)." *Box Office Mojo*. IMDb.com, Inc., n.d. Web. 7 Feb. 2015.

"Strays - Vin Diesel Interview." *IndieLondon*. IndieLondon.co.uk, n.d. Web. 7 Feb. 2015.

"Vin Diesel." *IMDb*. IMDB.com, Inc., n.d. Web. 07 Feb. 2015.

"Vin Diesel of The Chronicles of Riddick (Universal) Interview." Vin Diesel Source, n.d. Web. 07 Feb. 2015.

James Cameron

Goodyear, Dana. "Man of Extremes: The Return of James Cameron." *The New Yorker.* Condé Nast, 26 Oct. 2009. Web. 7 Feb. 2015.

"James Cameron Interview." *Academy of Achievement.* American Academy of Achievement, 18 June 1999. Web. 7 Feb. 2015.

Keegan, Rebecca. *The Futurist: The Life and Films of James Cameron.* New York: Crown, 2009. Print.

McGovern, Joe. "'The Terminator' at 30: An Oral History." *Entertainment Weekly.* Entertainment Weekly Inc., 17 July 2014. Web. 7 Feb. 2015.

"The Terminator (1984)." *Box Office Mojo.* IMDb.com, Inc., n.d. Web. 7 Feb. 2015.

Arnold Schwarzenegger

Lankester, Mark. "Arnold Schwarzenegger: The Weird Early Years." *Movie Editor's Blog.* Yahoo Movies, 24 Jan. 2013. Web. 7 Feb. 2015.

The Making of 'The Terminator': A Retrospective. Dir. Jeff McQueen. Perf. James Cameron and Arnold Schwarzenegger. Carolco Home Video, 1992.

Schwarzenegger, Arnold, and Peter Petre. *Total Recall: My Unbelievably True Life Story.* New York: Simon & Schuster, 2012. Print.

Martha Stewart

"Martha Stewart." *Bio.com*. A&E Television Networks, n.d. Web. 7 Feb. 2015.

"Martha Stewart Biography." *Academy of Achievement*. American Academy of Achievement, n.d. Web. 7 Feb. 2015.

John Grisham

Amazon Books. "How I Wrote It: An Interview with John Grisham." Online video clip. *YouTube*. YouTube, LLC, 26 Oct. 2014. Web. 7 Feb. 2015.

"Bio." *John Grisham*. Doubleday, Random House, Inc., n.d. Web. 7 Feb. 2015.

Brewer, Sonny. *Don't Quit Your Day Job: Acclaimed Authors and the Day Jobs They Quit*. 2nd ed. Douglas, Isle of Man: MP Publishing Limited, 2010. Print.

Grisham, John. "Boxers, Briefs and Books." *The New York Times*. The New York Times Company, 5 Sept. 2010. Web. 7 Feb. 2015.

"John Grisham: E-books Will Be Half of My Sales." *CBSNews*. CBS Interactive Inc., 11 Apr. 2012. Web. 7 Feb. 2015.

ReelFilmNews. "Origins of THE FIRM by John Grisham." Online video clip. *YouTube*. YouTube, LLC, 6 Apr. 2013. Web. 7 Feb. 2015.

Sir Richard Branson

"About Us." *Virgin.* Virgin.com, n.d. Web. 7 Feb. 2015.

Branson, Richard. *Losing My Virginity: How I've Survived, Had Fun, and Made a Fortune Doing Business My Way.* New York: Three Rivers Press, 1998. Print.

"Richard Branson." *Bloomberg Game Changers.* Bloomberg Television. 10 May 2011. Television.

Sylvester Stallone

Best Zonne. "Tony Robbins Tells Sylvester Stallone's Rags to Riches Story." Online video clip. *YouTube.* YouTube, LLC, 25 Nov. 2013. Web. 7 Feb. 2015.

Greene, Andy. "Flashback: Sylvester Stallone Stars in 1970 Softcore Porn Film." *Rolling Stone.* Rolling Stone, 14 Aug. 2014. Web. 7 Feb. 2015.

"Rocky (1976)." *Box Office Mojo.* IMDb.com, Inc., n.d. Web. 7 Feb. 2015.

"Sylvester Stallone." *Biography.* A&E Television Networks. 2 Mar. 2005. Television.

Jack Ma

Fannin, Rebecca. "How I Did It: Jack Ma, Alibaba.com: The Unlikely Rise of China's Hottest Internet Tycoon." *Inc.* Mansueto Ventures, 1 Jan. 2008. Web. 7 Feb. 2015.

Picker, Leslie, and Yilun Chen. "Alibaba's Banks Boost IPO Size to Record of $25 Billion." *Bloomberg Business*. Bloomberg L.P., 22 Sept. 2014. Web. 7 Feb. 2015.

Liu, Shiying, and Martha Avery. Alibaba: *The Inside Story behind Jack Ma and the Creation of the World's Biggest Online Marketplace*. New York: HarperCollins, 2009. Print.

Oprah Winfrey

"Behind the Scenes at Harpo Studios." *Oprah.com*. Harpo Productions, Inc., n.d. Web. 7 Feb. 2015.

Kelley, Kitty. *Oprah: A Biography*. New York: Crown, 2010. Print.

"Oprah Winfrey Interview." *Academy of Achievement*. American Academy of Achievement, n.d. Web. 7 Feb. 2015.

"OWN Unveils Original Programming for January 1, 2011, Launch" *Oprah.com*. Harpo Productions, Inc., 8 Apr. 2010. Web. 7 Feb. 2015.

Al Pacino

"Al Pacino: Inside Out." *Biography*. A&E Television Networks. 14 May 2001. Television.

"Al Pacino Lifetime." *Biography*. AETN UK, n.d. Web. 7 Feb. 2015.

Pacino, Al, and Lawrence Grobel. *Al Pacino in Conversation with Lawrence Grobel*. New York: Simon Spotlight Entertainment, 2006. Print.

Jon Hamm

Handy, Bruce. "Mad Men Q&A: Jon Hamm." *Vanity Fair*. Condé Nast, 5 Aug. 2009. Web. 7 Feb. 2015.

Iley, Chrissy. "The Interview: Jon Hamm." *The Guardian*. Guardian News and Media Limited, 27 Apr. 2008. Web. 7 Feb. 2015.

Lipworth, Elaine. "'I Was at the Very Bottom of the List': How Mad Men's Jon Hamm Finally Became a Leading Man." *MailOnline*. Associated Newspapers Ltd., 10 Mar. 2012. Web. 7 Feb. 2015.

Postman, Alex. "Jon Hamm." *Elle*. Hearst Communications, Inc., 21 Aug. 2009. Web. 7 Feb. 2015.

Jerry Seinfeld

"Jerry Seinfeld: Master of His Domain." *Biography*. A&E Television Networks. 11 May 1998. Television.

Oppenheimer, Jerry. *Seinfeld: The Making of an American Icon*. New York: HarperCollins, 2002. Print.

Tony Robbins

"About." *Tony Robbins*. Robbins Research International,

Inc., n.d. Web. 12 Feb. 2015.

"Tony Robbins: The Secret of His Success." *Biography.* A&E Television Networks. 3 Feb. 1999. Television.

Shania Twain

"Shania Twain." *Bio.com.* A&E Television Networks, n.d. Web. 7 Feb. 2015.

"Shania Twain." *Biography.* A&E Television Networks. 6 May 2005. Television.

Twain, Shania. *From This Moment On.* New York: Atria, 2011. Print.

Harrison Ford

"American Graffiti (1973)." *Box Office Mojo.* IMDb.com, Inc., n.d. Web. 7 Feb. 2015.

Duke, Brad. *Harrison Ford: The Films.* Jefferson, NC: McFarland, 2005. Print.

Thomas, Kate. "Star Wars Secrets Exposed: Why Harrison Ford Almost Missed out on

Han Solo Role and How R2-D2 Got His Name." Daily Mail. Associated Newspapers Ltd., 22 Sept. 2014. Web. 31 Mar. 2015.

Star Wars. "George Lucas Interview: Harrison Ford." Online video clip.

YouTube. YouTube, LLC, 01 Nov. 2013. Web. 1 Apr. 2015.

"Star Wars (1977)." Box Office Mojo. IMDb.com, Inc., n.d. Web. 1 Apr. 2015.

Charlize Theron

"Charlize Theron." *Bio.com*. A&E Television Networks, n.d. Web. 6 Feb. 2015.

"Charlize Theron." *Lifetime*. AETN UK, n.d. Web. 7 Feb. 2015.

Ellen DeGeneres

"Ellen Degeneres." *E! True Hollywood Story*. E! Entertainment Television, LLC. 4 Jan. 2004. Television.

James, Meg. "NBC Stations Renew 'The Ellen Degeneres Show' through 2017." *Los Angeles Times*. Tribune Publishing, 12 Mar. 2013. Web. 7 Feb. 2015.

Tyler Perry

"About Tyler." *TylerPerry.com*. Tyler Perry Studios, n.d. Web. 10 Feb. 2015.

Bowles, Scott. "Tyler Perry Holds on to His past." *USA Today*. Gannett Company, Inc., 9 Sept. 2008. Web. 7 Feb. 2015.

Pullery, Brett. "A Showbiz Whiz." *Forbes.com.* Forbes.com LLC, 15 Sept. 2005. Web. 7 Feb. 2015.

"Tyler Perry Studios." *TylerPerry.com.* Tyler Perry Studios, n.d. Web. 7 Feb. 2015.

"Tyler Perry's Diary of a Mad Black Woman (2005)." *Box Office Mojo.* IMDb.com, Inc., n.d. Web. 7 Feb. 2015.

"Tyler Perry's Oprah Show Retrospective." *Oprah.com.* Harpo Productions, Inc., 20 Oct. 2010. Web. 7 Feb. 2015.

Henry Ford

"Henry Ford." *History.com.* A&E Television Networks, n.d. Web. 1 Feb. 2015.

Ford, Henry, and Samuel Crowther. *My Life and Work.* Garden City, NY: Doubleday, 1922. Print.

"Timeline. Henry Ford. American Experience. WGBH." *American Experience.* WGBH Educational Foundation, n.d. Web. 7 Feb. 2015.

Watts, Steven. The People's Tycoon: Henry Ford and the American Century. New York: A.A. Knopf, 2005. Print.

David Neeleman

"Dados Comparativos Avançados" (in Portuguese). Agência Nacional de Aviação Civil (ANAC). 29 May 2013. Web. 7 Feb. 2015.

"David Neeleman." *Bloomberg Risk Takers*. Bloomberg Television. 12 July 2011. Television.

Wynbrandt, James. Flying High: How JetBlue Founder and CEO David Neeleman Beats the Competition... Even in the World's Most Turbulent Industry. Hoboken, NJ: Wiley, 2006. Print.

Mark Cuban

Burke, Monte. "At Age 25 Mark Cuban Learned Lessons About Leadership That Changed His Life." *Forbes.com*. Forbes.com LLC, 28 Mar. 2013. Web. 7 Feb. 2015.

Cuban, Mark. *How to Win at the Sport of Business: If I Can Do It, You Can Do It*. New York: Diversion, 2011. Print.

Cuban, Mark. "Success and Motivation, Part 2." *Blog Maverick | the Mark Cuban Weblog*. Mark Cuban, 25 Apr. 2004. Web. 7 Feb. 2015.

Swisher, Kara and Evan Ramstad. "Yahoo! to Announce Acquisition Of Broadcast.com for $5.7 Billion." *The Wall Street Journal*. Dow Jones & Company, Inc., 1 Apr. 1999. Web. 7 Feb. 2015.

"Mark Cuban." *Bloomberg Game Changers*. Bloomberg Television. 2012. Television.

Swartz, Jon. "Losing's Not an Option for Cuban." *USA Today*. Gannett Company, Inc., 25 Apr. 2004. Web. 7 Feb. 2015.

Jay Z

"Jay-Z." *Bloomberg Risk Takers*. Bloomberg Television. 18 Nov. 2010. Television.

"Jay-Z's Reasonable Doubt By the Numbers." *XXL Magazine*. Townsquare Media, Inc., 25 June 2011. Web. 7 Feb. 2015.

Ross, Erik. "The 50 Best Selling Rap Albums of All Time." *Complex*. Complex Media Inc., 18 May 2013. Web. 7 Feb. 2015.

Ursula Burns

Business Strategy Review. "Profile: Ursula Burns, CEO and Chairman, Xerox Corporation." Online video clip. *YouTube*. YouTube, LLC, 14 Feb. 2012. Web. 7 Feb. 2015.

Iqbal, Muneeza. "The Makers: Xerox CEO Ursula Burns Tells Her Story." *Daily Finance*. AOL Inc., 25 Feb. 2013. Web. 7 Feb. 2015.

"Ursula Burns, Chairman and CEO of Xerox Corporation." *Xerox*. Xerox Corporation, n.d. Web. 7 Feb. 2015.

John D. Rockefeller, Sr.

Chernow, Ron. *Titan: The Life of John D. Rockefeller, Sr.* New York: Random House, 1998. Print.

"John D. Rockefeller." *Bio.com*. A&E Television Networks, n.d. Web. 7 Feb. 2015.

"John D. Rockefeller, Senior." *American Experience*. WGBH Educational Foundation, n.d. Web. 7 Feb. 2015.

O'Donnell, Carl. "The Rockefellers: The Legacy Of History's Richest Man." *Forbes.com*. Forbes.com LLC, 11 July 2014. Web. 7 Feb. 2015.

Segall, Grant. *John D. Rockefeller: Anointed with Oil*. New York: Oxford University Press, 2001. Print.

Stevens, Mark. Rich is a Religion: Breaking the Timeless Code to Wealth. Hoboken, NJ: Wiley, 1999. Print.

Howard Schultz

Schultz, Howard, and Dori Jones Yang. Pour Your Heart into It: How Starbucks Built a

Company One Cup at a Time. New York: Hyperion, 1997. Print.

"Company Information." Starbucks Coffee Company. Starbucks Corporation, n.d. Web. 7 Feb. 2015.

CPSIA information can be obtained
at www.ICGtesting.com
Printed in the USA
LVOW13s0257200217

524789LV00008B/369/P